ON THE WIN

VOLUME 01: THE BEGINNING O

MW00895973

Written & Edited By: Allan Udy

Chief Photographer: Alex Mitchell

Additional Contributors
The Vintage Aviator Ltd
Les Bushell   Kim Harris
Thomas Fedor   Rob Leigh
Sid Mosdell   Leo Pardon
Stefan Pinczolits
Alex Robinson (www.alexrobinson.co.nz)
Tim Sullivan   Daniel Werner

Photos inside the Omaka Aviation Heritage Centre are reproduced here-in with the permission of the New Zealand Aviation Museum Trust.

Design/Layout/Publishing

Historical Aviation Film Unit

A Division of
Golden Micro Solutions Ltd,
P.O. Box 590, Blenheim, NZ.
www.golden.co.nz

Printing
Kalamazoo Wyatt & Wilson
Christchurch, New Zealand
www.wyatt-wilson.co.nz

ISBN   978-0-473-16677-9

Cover Photo: Reproduction Royal Aircraft Factory F.E.2b built by The Vintage Aviator Ltd.
Pilot: Gene De Marco
Gunner: Lee Bennett

Back Cover Photo: Reproduction Albatros D.Va built by The Vintage Aviator Ltd. *Pilot* Gene De Marco

Inside Cover Photo (at left): The sharp end of the Albatros D.Va.

Historical Aviation Film Unit
www.aviationfilm.com

Forewo...

We've always enjoyed watching historic aircraft do their thing, and in the final decade of the 20th Century we attended several Warbirds Over Wanaka shows in Wanaka, New Zealand. The range of aircraft at these shows was huge, and for guys who grew up on a staple diet of World War 2 movies, comics and books, the heavy metal of the fighter aircraft on display was simply awesome. We saw Spitfires, Me.109s, Corsairs, P40 Kittyhawks, P51 Mustangs, Polikapov's, Yak's, a Grumman Avenger, and even a restored Battle of Britain veteran Hawker Hurricane.

What we rarely saw was aircraft from the pioneering days of flight and the First World War—primarily because there were virtually no such aircraft in New Zealand at the time. Stuart Tantrum had built a full size replica Fokker Dr.1 Triplane in 1985 (ZK-FOK), and this was seen on the local airshow circuit periodically. Stuart also built a Replica Plans 7/10ths version of the Royal Aircraft Factory S.E.5a (subsequently destroyed in an accident in Auckland) while a second Replica Plans S.E.5a belonging to Tom Grant from Dunedin was periodically seen at the Wanaka shows. The only other pre-1920 aircraft that were seen in New Zealand were the visiting 1911 Blériot XI and 1919 Thumilisa owned by Swedish pilot Mikael Carlson which were displayed at the 1998 Warbirds Over Wanaka show.

In the 21st Century things were destined to change. By January 2001 plans were well in hand for the first Classic Fighters airshow to be held at Omaka Aerodrome in Blenheim. In addition to the WW2-era aircraft to be displayed at the show it was rumored that we'd also see a new WW1 type—a recently imported full size Sopwith Camel with an authentic rotary engine. The organisers subsequently went one

Sopwith Camel, 2001

better by convincing American owner/builder Ed Storo to bring his Bristol Fighter F.2b replica to the show as well. These two imports, along with Stuart's Fokker Dr.1 meant that the first Classic Fighters show boasted an incredible *three* full size WW1 aircraft—something not seen here since the late 1930s.

After the 2001 show the F.2b stayed in New Zealand and along with the Camel and Triplane, formed the nucleus of what was to eventually become a major collection of aircraft operated and (in some cases) built by The Vintage Aviator Ltd, on behalf of the 1914-1918 Aviation Heritage Trust. From that small beginning the collection has grown at a rate which was not even imagined at the dawn of the century.

Over the years some aircraft have come and gone while others have had their appearance altered at some point. This book is a record of all the Collection's aircraft and their colour schemes seen in the first decade of the 21st Century—we hope this inspires an interest in and appreciation for these World War One-era aircraft, as they've done for us.   *Allan Udy & Alex Mitchell*

Aviation - The First Fifteen Years

For scores of years before the 20th Century, man had been trying to defy gravity in order to soar through the air like a bird. By the start of the century, hot air balloons had been in use for some time and rudimentary gliders had been used for short flights. But the prize that was powered and controlled flight in heavier-than-air craft still proved elusive.

At the start of 1903 the beginning of powered aviation was only a few months away. Many pioneers were developing their designs for what they hoped would be the first successful aircraft in these months, but none of them realised that in only fifteen short years mankind would go from being flightless to being able to fly halfway around the world, and that aviation would evolve from being a curiosity to a world wide industry and new combat arm of the military.

This section of the book is not intended to be a detailed work on the history and development of aviation during its infancy. It is however intended to give the uninitiated reader a taste and understanding of the scale and rate of technical advances made in aviation during this period.

1903 - Wright Flyer at Kitty Hawk, N.C.

1903

It is reputed that on 31st March, New Zealander Richard Pearse made a powered flight of around 45m in a monoplane aircraft of his own construction. This was followed by a flight of around 900m in May, but like the earlier flight, documentary evidence is lacking and Pearse is generally not regarded as the father of flight. Instead, on the 17th of December 1903, on a windswept beach at Kitty Hawk, North Carolina (USA), Orville and Wilbur Wright became the first people to pilot a powered heavier-than-air craft in a sustained and controlled manner. At 10:35AM, Orville (lying prone) piloted the craft a distance of over 36m in 12 seconds. Three further flights were made later that same day. As seen in the photograph above, this aircraft did not have wheels, but rather was launched into the wind after running along a timber rail. The aircraft was damaged late in the day after being picked up by wind and never flew again.

1904

In April Gabriel Voisin made a number of successful glider flights in France. In August the first successful US Airship (California Arrow) was demonstrated in California, while in November Wilbur Wright flew the 'Flyer II' a distance of some three miles, near Dayton, Ohio. This feat was the first ever flight of more than five minutes.

1905

Many aviation pioneers such as Samuel Cody and Voisin were still experimenting with airships, gliders and kites capable of lifting a passenger. By September the Wrights were regularly flying the 'Flyer III' for more than twenty minutes at a time. In November the first German Zeppelin (airship) was damaged during its first launch.

1906

In March, Romania inventor Traian Vuia became the first person to design, build and fly a heavier-than-

air craft in Europe. The aircraft (seen below) flew a distance of 12m before the engine failed. Later in the year several other pioneers flew their aircraft for the first time, including Brazilian Alberto Santos-Dumont who won the Archdeacon Prize when he became the first person in France to fly an aircraft more than 25m (he flew 60m). Several Zeppelins made their maiden flights and the first Gordon Bennett Cup for ballooning was won by an American who flew 647km in his US Army balloon.

1907

During 1907 the first flights were made in the UK, an Aeronautical Division was formed within the U.S. Army Signal Corps, and in France Léon Delagrange flew one of the first of many Voisin designed aircraft a distance of 10m. Robert Esnault-Pelterie became the first pilot to fly using a control stick rather than a wheel, and Louis Blériot designed several aircraft. The Blériot VI became the worlds first successful monoplane, and was essentially the first design resembling modern aircraft.

1906 - Traian Vuia

1908 - Wright Model A

1908

By the end of 1908, Wilbur Wright had flown a world record distance of 123km (in one flight), the first passengers had been flown in aircraft, the U.S. Army announced plans to purchase a number of aircraft, and the first aviation fatality was recorded when Orville Wright crashed the *Wright Model A* (above) killing his passenger. During the year many names that were to become synonymous with aviation began to emerge as new aircraft were built and first flights made— these included Henry Farman, Glenn Curtiss, Alliot Verdon Roe, the Short Brothers and Samuel Cody. It was this year that Orville Wright made the remark that

"No flying machine will ever fly from New York to Paris ... [because] no known motor can run at the requisite speed for four days without stopping."

1909

In July Louis Blériot made headlines by being the first person to make an aerial crossing of the English Channel. Flying a Blériot XI (*seen below in the form of Mikael Carlson's replica*) the crossing from France took only 37 minutes. First flights were also made in Canada and Australia, Samuel Cody made the first cross-country flight in the UK (Aldershot to Farnborough return), and the first airline was formed in Germany. In August Glen Curtiss won a major prize at the First International Air Races held in Reims, and in November Alec Ogilvie patented the first airspeed indicator.

1910

In January the 1910 Los Angeles International Air Meet, the first aviation meeting in the USA was held. By April the French Air Force (*Aviation Militaire*) had

been formed, and in July, Bert Pither is thought to have flown the first metal framed aircraft at Riverton in New Zealand (see overleaf). Other events this year included the first flight over the Alps, the sending of the first aircraft-to-ground radio message, the first solo flight in the USA by a female, and the first commercial freight flight in the USA.

The Bristol Boxkite, an improved version of a Henry Farman design, made its first flight in July while in September the single example of the Roe IV Triplane built by Alliot Verdon Roe had its maiden flight.

During 1910 the Deperdussin Monoplane was flown for the first time. This aircraft would eventually become the Deperdussin TT model which was used by both the Royal Flying Corps and French *Aviation Militaire* in small numbers prior to the outbreak of war in 1914.

1910 - Blériot XI replica (Carlson)

1910 - Pither replica airborne at Classic Fighters 2005

1911

In January the first aircraft to land on a ship (*USS Pennsylvania*) did so in San Francisco Harbour, while the first undisputed flight in New Zealand was made by Vivian Walsh in a Howard Wright biplane. The Spanish Air Force was founded in March and in the following month the Air Battalion of the Royal Engineers was formed making it the first British military aviation unit. The US Naval Aviation Service was created in May and later that year airmail flights were made for the first time.

In October the first military use of an aircraft was made when an Italian Blériot XI was used to spy on Turkish forces duing the Italo-Turkish War. A month later another first was made when an Italian aircraft dropped bombs on Turkish troops.

1912

This was the year in which military aviation really started to develop. The Bulgarian Air Force was formed (with 23 aircraft), the first flights were made from the decks of ships, Anthony Fokker formed his first company to build aircraft and the Royal Flying Corps was formed in June. In the same month the Sopwith Aviation company was founded, the Lewis machine gun was tested on an aircraft for the first time, and Lt Hans Dons made the first flight in Norway in an Etrich Taube (*see page 50*). By the end of the year the Australian Flying Corps had been formed, as had the Danish Air Force, the Argentine Air Force and the Italian Air Battalion. While flying a Deperdussin monoplane in February, Jules Vedrines became the first pilot to exceed 100 mph (161 km/h) in flight.

1913

In February a Russian flying for Greece became the first pilot to be shot down (during the First Balkan War) when his aircraft was hit by ground fire.

In April the first Schneider Trophy contest for seaplanes was staged. The race offered a large prize pool and was designed to encourage technical advances in aviation—the contest was run 11 times up until 1931.

By July the U.S. Army has formed the 1st Aero Squadron, the Brazilian Navy had formed a flying school, the Chilean Air Force had been established, the Royal Netherlands Army had developed an Aviation Division and China had purchased twelve military aircraft from France.

By the end of the year the first parachute jump from an aircraft

1910 - Deperdussin (Shuttleworth Collection, UK)

had been completed, an aircraft was flown inverted for the first time, and Roland Garros made the first aerial crossing of the Mediterranean in just under 8 hours.

During the year some notable aircraft designs were developed, one of which was the Avro 504—a type that was to become one of the training mainstays of the Royal Flying Corps until the end of the First World War. The Sopwith Tabloid first flew in December 1913 and became the first of many significant and formidable fighter designs by the Sopwith Aviation company—36 Tabloids entered service with the Royal Flying Corps and the Royal Naval Air Service at the outbreak of war in 1914. In December the Russian-built Sikorsky Ilya Muromets was flown for the first time. This mammoth aircraft (with a 30m wingspan) was the worlds first four-engined bomber and up to 1918 over 70 were built.

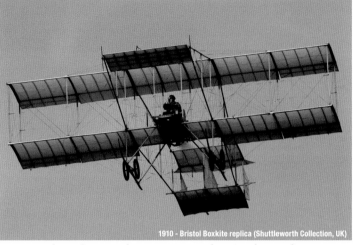
1910 - Bristol Boxkite replica (Shuttleworth Collection, UK)

1914

Early in the year an Ilya Muromets set a new record by lifting 16 people to a height of 2000m, and in March the Royal Siamese Flying Corps was formed. Howard Paxton won the Schneider Trophy contest in Monaco flying a seaplane variant of the Sopwith Tabloid averaging 139 km/h over the triangular course.

July the 28th marked the beginning of the First World War, and the beginning of over four years of intense aviation related research and development as each combatant nation strove to develop faster and more powerful aircraft.

In August a French observer became the first aviation casualty of the war when he was shot by ground fire. A Royal Aircraft Factory B.E.2 operated by the Royal Flying Corp became the first British aircraft to arrive in France, and in that same month an Avro 504 was shot down by German rifle fire becoming the first RFC aircraft destroyed in action. Later in the month Paris was bombed for the first time by a German crew flying an Etrich Taube.

In October two Frenchmen flying a Voisin III became the first flyers to score an air-to-air victory when they used their machine gun to shoot down a German Aviatik B.II observation aircraft. The Royal Naval Air Service undertook the first strategic air raid on Germany when two Sopwith Tabloid aircraft were tasked with attacking Zeppelin sheds at Düsseldorf.

1911 - Avro Triplane IV replica (Shuttleworth Collection, UK)

1912 - Blackburn monoplane Type 'D' (Shuttleworth Collection, UK)

The following month three RNAS Avro 504s attacked the Zeppelin sheds at Friedrichshafen.

By the end of December, Britain has been bombed for the first time when a Taube dropped two bombs in Kent.

1915

Early in the year several nations continued to experiment with the use of aircraft for bombing—the German Navy staged its first Zeppelin raid on the UK, several Russian Ilya Muromets bombed targets in Poland and the British used aircraft for tactical bombing in support of ground troops in Flanders.

By mid-year Roland Garros had made the first air-to-air kill using a forward facing machine gun firing through the propeller arc, and the first Zeppelin to be destroyed in an air-to-air combat was bombed by an RNAS Morane-Saulnier Type L.

In July the first aerial victory by a true fighter aircraft occurred when Kurt Wintgens shot down a Morane-Saulnier using the prototype Fokker Eindecker. The acknowledged 'father' of fighter pilots, Oswald Boelcke claimed his first victory in the same month while in August Max Immelman made his first kill.

Technical advances in the latter part of the year included the first aircraft attack on a ship with an air-launched torpedo, the first take-off from a ship

with a wheeled undercarriage, and the initial flight of the first practical all-metal aircraft, the German Junkers J.1.

During the year several other famous aircraft types were introduced into service, including the Vickers Gunbus F.B.5 in February, the Morane-Saulnier Type N in April, and the Royal Aircraft Factory F.E.2 in September.

1916

Importantly for the Allies the Airco DH.2 entered service in February 1916, giving them an aircraft with which to begin to neutralise the 'Fokker Scourge'— the Fokker Eindecker had given the Germans the advantage in the air war since mid-1915.

In March the US military used aircraft to fly their first mission over foreign soil when several Curtiss JN3 aircraft were used for reconnaissance over Mexico.

A month later the British used aircraft for the first aerial re-supply mission when they delivered 13 tons of supplies to Kut el Amara (in Mesopotamia), while it was besieged by the Turks.

In April the Lafayette Escadrille was established as an American volunteer unit in France. In June Victor Chapman from that unit became the first American airman to be killed in action.

In July the Battle of the Somme began, and over the next five months the British lost 782 aircraft and over 500 hundred pilots (however they retained air superiority over the battlefield). In August 16 German Zeppelins raided the south-east of England, and Lt Leefe-Robinson shot one down while flying a Royal Aircraft Factory B.E.2c. During the same moth German ace Oswald Boelcke formed the first specialised German fighter unit—Jagdstaffel (Jasta) 2.

1913 - Royal Aircraft Factory S.E.2 (Scout Experimental)

During September a British submarine was sunk by Austrian Lohner flying boats, becoming the first such vessel to be destroyed by aircraft. Also this month, Manfred von Richthofen shot down his first aircraft while flying an Albatros D.II.

Aircraft developments continued apace throughout the year with the Sopwith 1 1/2 Strutter entering service in April, the SPAD S.VII in August, the Sopwith Triplane in November.

1915 - Airco DH.1

1917

In response to continued Zeppelin raids on England, the RFC formed No 100 Sqn, the first British specialist night fighter unit in January. During 'Bloody April' the RFC lost 245 aircraft from a total of 365 during the Arras offensive. That same month the United States declared war on Germany and entered the conflict.

In May, Frenchman René Fonck shot down six German aircraft in one day, the US adopted their 'star in a circle' national insignia, an RNAS flying boat sunk a German submarine, and the Germans staged a massed air raid against targets in Kent with 21 Gotha G.V bombers.

In August a Sopwith Pup made the first aircraft landing on a moving ship (HMS Furious), and the following month the US 1st Aero Squadron arrived in France. Later in the month René Fonck shot down six German aircraft in one day, for the second time!

During the year the Airco DH.4 entered service, as did the Royal

Aircraft Factory S.E.5 in March. The Bristol Fighter equipped No 48 Sqn in April and in June the Sopwith Camel entered service.

1918

In February the Lafayette Escadrille was transferred from the French Army to the US Army and was renamed the 103rd Aero. The Finnish Air Force was founded in March and in the same month the first successful powered heavier-than-air unmanned craft flight was made when a Curtiss-Sperry Flying Bomb was tested. Also in this month the first regular international air mail service began (between Austria and the Ukraine), the first Norwegian airline was founded, the US Navy made its first aerial attack on an enemy submarine and Capt J Trollope of the RFC shot down six enemy aircraft in one day.

In April the RFC and RNAS were combined to form the Royal Air Force, while the highest scoring ace of the war, Manfred von Richthofen was shot down and killed. The final Zeppelin raids on England were made that month.

In May the first scheduled US airmail service (between Washington and New York) began, while the Canadian equivalent (Montreal to Toronto) started in June. Also in June the RAF used its new 1650lb bomb for the first time when one was dropped in Belgium.

In August a German fighter pilot made the first combat use of a parachute to escape from his burning Pfalz D.III fighter (British pilots were not issued with parachutes until after 1918). By the Armistice in November the RAF had suffered some 16600 casualties, while the German Air Service also suffered in excess of 15000.

The end of the war saw a huge number of military aircraft become surplus to requirements, and many of these were used for new civilian pioneering activities. A Handley Page O/400 bomber was used to survey an airmail route from Greece to India, while the first England-India flight was made in a Handley Page V/1500, which had been initially designed as a heavy bomber with which the British could attack Berlin from bases in England's East Anglia.

In the space of only fifteen short years aviation had advanced from those first small hops in the Wright's Flyer at Kitty Hawk, to aircraft like the V/1500 sporting a wingspan of 38m and four 375hp engines, which gave the aircraft an endurance of 17 hours and a range of over 2000km—all while carrying a bomb load of up to 3400kg! ❖

1915 - Air Department (AD) Scout 'Sparrow'

The Vintage Aviator

The Vintage Aviator Ltd (TVAL) is a New Zealand Civil Aviation Authority (CAA) approved aircraft restoration and manufacturing company.

The main aim of the company is to build World War One-era aircraft, engines and propellers to the same exacting standards they were originally made in the early years of the 20th Century. In this regard the company is almost unique in the world aviation community as few other manufacturing companies specialise solely in the 1914-1918 period.

TVAL endeavours to maintain absolute authenticity with the original designs, making both airworthy and static aircraft for museum display and private collections.

In addition to construction, the company's engineers also look after, and operate, the World War One aircraft owned by the 1914-1918 Aviation Heritage Trust.

The Vintage Aviator works closely with the New Zealand CAA to fulfil it's obligations as a certified aircraft manufacturer, and in May 2007 gained its CAA approval and Part 148 Manufacturing Organisation Certificate (the aviation industry equivalent to the ISO 9001 2000 standard).

TVAL staff have a great deal to be proud of, a state of the art manufacturing facility coupled with an ICAO Aircraft Manufacturing approval. These two remarkable achievements emphasize their commitment to engineering excellence and technical innovation. They use the most modern technology to reproduce the most accurate aircraft reproductions from a bygone era.

The company's facilities in Wellington and at Hood Aerodrome in Masterton are capable of every imaginable aspect of aircraft and engine construction.

The company's single most valuable resource is their skilled craftsmen—specialized woodworkers, welders and machin-ists, and people experienced in the complexities of fabric covered aircraft. This is the first time since World War One that these aircraft are being produced in a factory setting.

Despite using traditional and authentic materials and techniques, the company also utilises the most modern CNC and CAD technology to increase accuracy and reduce labour costs. Working relationships with other restoration facilities and museums in Europe, Australia, Canada and in the USA assists TVAL in sourcing information as well as technical data and original parts for duplication and reproduction.

See the TVAL web site at:
www.thevintageaviator.com ❖

Knights Of The Sky Exhibition At Omaka

In the late 1990s two highly successful warbird 'fly-ins' were held at Omaka Aerodrome (Blenheim, New Zealand) and it became apparent that the local populace were developing a growing interest in vintage and warbird aviation.

This resulted in the formation of the New Zealand Aviation Museum Trust* tasked to build and run a museum at Omaka, and the formation of the Classic Fighters Airshow Charitable Trust, to run a biennial airshow to raise funds for the museum. After successful airshows in 2001, 2003 and 2005 the new Omaka Aviation Heritage Centre (OAHC) was officially opened on the 8th December 2006.

de Havilland DH.4

The initial plan was that the first hangar area would house some of the WW1 aircraft belonging to the 1914-1918 Aviation Heritage Trust, while the second would be used to display other historic aircraft based at Omaka.

However, as the size of the 1914-1918 Trusts' collection grew, it became apparent that initially the museum could concentrate solely on aircraft of the period up to the end of WW1. To this end the museum now houses the 'Knights Of The Sky' exhibition—a fascinating presentation of static and fly-able aircraft, and memorabilia from the period 1910 to 1918.

On display are over 20 full size aircraft of the period, from the two well preserved original aircraft, the Caproni Ca.22 and

de Havilland DH.4, through to new-build reproductions of the Royal Aircraft Factory S.E.5a and R.E.8. Between these extremes is an amazing range of Great War aircraft types from well known (at the time) companies such as Fokker, Bristol, Pfalz, Halberstadt, Nieuport, Airco, Siemens and Morane-Saulnier.

In addition to the aircraft is the incredible display of early aviation memorabilia. A flying suit belonging to US ace Eddie Rickenbacker features, as does Frenchman René Fonck's *Croix de Guerre* and Ernst Udet's *Blue Max*. Items belonging to the German aces Oswald Boelcke and Max Immelman are also displayed, as are many items of insignia salvaged from crashed aircraft—in particular items from the Lafayette Escadrille (featured in the movie *Fly Boys*). In a separate area adjacent to a life size diorama of Manfred von Richthofen's crashed Fokker Dr.1 Triplane is the display of von Richthofen family memorabilia. This collection includes the actual cross cut from von Richthofen's crashed aircraft, trophies belonging to both Manfred and his brother Lothar, their father Albrecht's dress uniform, and many other unique artifacts that once belonged to the family.

This is not a run-of-the-mill hangar display with two rows of aircraft parked closely together in roped off enclosures. Instead the aircraft are displayed as part of numerous full size dioramas put together by the team from Wingnut Films and Weta Workshops in Wellington (the same team that

Omaka
Aviation Heritage Centre

created many of the visual effects for the *Lord of the Rings*, and other Hollywood blockbusters). Amongst other sights portrayed are the ground crew extracting a wounded pilot from a British aircraft just as a Model T Ford field ambulance arrives amidst the mud of the airfield; the crew of an Allied two-seater

checking their navigation while armourers on the ground finish rearming their guns; a German pilot talking to an Englishman he's just shot down (the German having landed his aircraft on a snow covered field); and New Zealand ace 'Grid' Caldwell about to leap into the mud of the front line trenches from the wing of his damaged Royal Aircraft Factory S.E.5a.

The Centre is open from 10:00AM to 4:00PM, 363 days a year. Find out more about the museum and which aircraft are currently on display at: *www.omaka.org.nz* ❖

* Note this is not the same organisation as the 1914-1918 Aviation Heritage Trust

Caproni Ca.22

Hood Flying Displays

Some old aircraft collections are only displayed inside vast hangars well away from the weather, but this is not the case with the aircraft of the 1914-1918 Aviation Heritage Trust and The Vintage Aviator collection.

Through the first decade of the 21st Century many of these aircraft were seen at a variety of shows and displays around New Zealand—Warbirds Over Wanaka, Classic Fighters Marlborough, Warbirds Over Wairarapa and other smaller events.

However, given that the reproduction aircraft on display are becoming even more authentic, and due to the growing size of the collection, TVAL now runs its own aerial displays at Hood Aerodrome in Masterton (New Zealand), where the airworthy aircraft are based.

The World War One aircraft based at Hood represent the largest, airworthy collection in New Zealand and they're able to be operated at the Aerodrome due to the fact that it is contains a large grass airfield, has a relative absence of paved surfaces, and the unrestricted airspace above the field and within the immediate area that allows these non-radio equipped aircraft to operate safely.

Remembrance Day

The Armistice agreement between the Allies and Germany to cease the hostilities of World War One was signed in a railway carriage in the Compiègne Forest at 5:00AM on the 11th of November 1918, and was scheduled to take effect at 11:00AM that same day.

The signing of the agreement was the end of a process that had begun in late September 1918 when the German High Command initially informed

Kaiser Wilhelm II that the military situation on the Western Front was hopeless and that the Allies were likely to be able to break through the German lines. While the signing of the agreement represented a defeat for Germany, it stopped short of being a totally unconditional surrender.

The first flying display day of the season is usually run on the Saturday closest to Remembrance Day (11th of November).

This is a chance to get the aircraft out of the hangar after a winter lay-over, and it's also an opportunity to remind the public of the significance of the 11th November—the date that marked the end of what was known as The War To End All Wars.

Joyeux Noel

The Wings Over Wairarapa airshow is held at Hood Aerodrome, in January every second year. On alternate (even) years between these major shows, a second TVAL display of the season is run in late January.

This is a chance to recall and celebrate the 'Joyeux Noel' events of December 1914.

By late December 1914, having endured over five months of indecisive warfare, both Allied and German troops on the Western Front were already feeling war-weary, and despite public calls for an end to the conflict, there was no official truce. However from Christmas Eve through until New Years Day (in some sectors of the front) an unofficial cessation of hostilities took place. In many areas this included troops from both sides meeting in 'No Man's Land' to celebrate the season of goodwill. This is a timely reminder that even in times of war the good aspects of human nature can often prevail.

ANZAC Day

The final display of the season is usually run on the Saturday closest to Anzac Day on April 25th. This anniversary commemorates the day in April 1915 that Australian and New Zealand troops, along with Allies from other nations, landed at Gallipoli in Turkey in an ill-fated attempt to control the waterways of the Dardenelles. The campaign was designed to secure the route from the Aegean Sea (east of Greece) through the Bosporus into the Black Sea, providing a naval link between the Allies and Russia. After almost eight months of intense fighting the Allies finally admitted defeat at the hands of the Turkish defenders and withdrew from the area.

Anzac Day, and this final display of the season is an opportunity to remember the 45,000 Allied soldiers killed during the campaign, and more importantly to remember all Australian and New Zealand servicemen and women who have served their country.

All the flying displays at Hood begin in the early afternoon, and run for several hours. The public first get the chance to take a (very) close up look at all the aircraft on the display line, and if they're lucky, take the opportunity to talk to some of the pilots and maintenance staff of these fascinating old aircraft. Additionally, there's often a variety of authentic and replica vintage motor vehicles on the field, and in some cases the public are encouraged to partake in a joy-ride or two in these vehicles.

By mid-afternoon the flying programme proper gets underway, and public is transported back in time—not only getting the chance to see these pioneering military aircraft, but to hear them (with many of the aircraft sporting original WW1-era engines), and also to *smell* them—an often overlooked facet of early aviation.

The growing public interest and awareness in these two major WW1 anniversaries (Anzac and Remembrance Days), the growing collection of aircraft based at Hood Aerodrome, and the ease of running low key flying events, means that these are likely to continue on a regular basis.

Keep your eye on the TVAL website for exact details of up and coming flying events: *www.thevintageaviator.com*

Hangar Tours

In addition to the official flying display days, the aircraft of The Vintage Aviator collection are also available for public viewing by way of static hangar tours.

Throughout the summer months, November through April, the hangar housing the collection at Hood Aerodrome is open to the public each Saturday and Sunday between 10:00AM and 4:00PM. One hour guided tours occur at 11:00AM, 1:00PM and 3:00PM.

In addition to the World War One aircraft, you'll also get to see a number of other aircraft during these open days. Of particular note are the Goodyear FG-1D Corsair and the Curtiss P40 Kittyhawk—both of which are amongst the last surviving airworthy RNZAF aircraft to see combat and be flown by New Zealanders during the Second World War.

Private tours are available to groups of ten or more adults at any time of the year by prior arrangement. If you want to organise and book a tour contact TVAL on their Info Line (06 370 2304), or by email at: *info@tval.co.nz* ❖

Fokker Dr.1 'Triplane'

107 / 17 Lt. von Conta

Built in 1985 this replica was the first full size World War One-era aircraft flown in New Zealand for several decades. For many years the aircraft was seen at airshows and displays up and down the country in this five-lozenge pattern colour scheme, representative of aircraft of the German Army Air Service.

However, while many German aircraft did wear this type of scheme (in which the lozenge pattern was actually printed onto the fabric, and not painted), the original Fokker Dr.1s built in this period did not use this colourful scheme. Rather they were painted in a streaky pattern (as seen elsewhere in this book).

Despite the slightly spurious colour scheme of this replica, the aircraft was intended to represent Dr.1 107/17 which was delivered from the Schwerin factory to Jasta 11 on the Western Front in October 1917. This aircraft (107/17) was one of the first production Dr.1s built and appears to have had a relatively long service life as it was still operational with Jasta 11 as late as March 1918, apparently as the personal aircraft of Lt. von Conta.

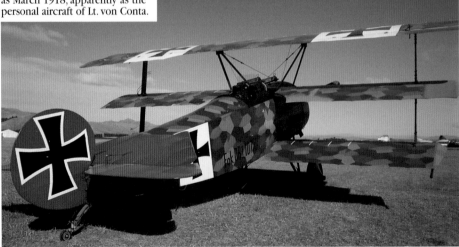

Year: 1917   *Built:* 320   *Top Speed:* 185km/h   *Operational Ceiling:* 6100m   *Wingspan:* 7.19m   *Height:* 2.95m   *Length:* 5.77m
Max Weight: 586kg   *Engine:* 110hp Le Rhône rotary   *Climb:* 5.7m/s   *Range:* 300km   *Armament:* 2 x 7.92mm Spandau LMG
This Aircraft: Replica with a 220hp Continental radial engine, built in NZ in 1985 by Stuart Tantrum and John Lanham. *ZK-FOK*

Facing Page Pilot: John Lanham

Sopwith F.1 Camel

B3889 - Capt. Clive Collett

The Camel is almost certainly the most well known and recognised Allied aircraft of the First World War. This fame is well deserved as it is also arguably the most successful of all the Allied fighter designs to emerge during the war years.

Herbert Smith, Sopwith's main aircraft designer, had his first major success with the Sopwith Pup in 1915, and followed this with the Sopwith Triplane in 1916 (though less than 200 of these latter aircraft were built). In 1917 Smith developed his first aircraft armed with twin machine guns, the Biplane F.1, which due to the humped fairing over the machine guns, unofficially became known as the 'Camel'.

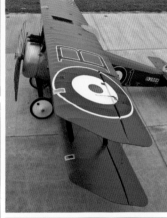

The type was credited with destroying more enemy aircraft than any other Allied aircraft.

Since its NZ debut at the Classic Fighters Marlborough 2001 airshow this Camel has worn the colour scheme of Marlborough-born ace Capt. Clive Collett who was the first Allied pilot to score a victory while flying a Camel. Having amassed a total of 12 victories Collett was killed while test flying a captured German Albatros aircraft in 1917.

Year: 1917 *Built:* 5490 *Top Speed:* 182 km/h *Operational Ceiling:* 5790m *Wingspan:* 8.53m *Height:* 2.6m *Length:* 5.72m
Max Weight: 659kg *Engine:* 80hp Gnome rotary *Climb:* 5.5m/s *Range:* 485km *Endurance:* 150mins *Armament:* 2 x .303
Vickers with provision for four 9kg bombs *This Aircraft:* Replica with original 160hp Gnome engine, built in the USA. ZK-JMU

Facing Page Pilot: Gene De Marco

Bristol Fighter F.2b

A Flight (red-white-red fuselage band), No. 2 Sqn RAF, 1920. The original F.2b s/n J7624 was not a No. 2 Sqn aircraft.

Shipped to NZ from the USA for the Classic Fighters 2001 airshow, this replica was later bought by the 1914-1918 Aviation Heritage Trust and has remained in New Zealand ever since.

The F.2b was arguably the most successful two-seater of World War One. With its high speed, ability to carry a worthwhile bomb load, and boasting the agility of a fighter, it set the standard for what would subsequently be referred to as fighter-bombers.

The 'Brisfit' was so successful that a number of Royal Air Force squadrons continued to use the type for a decade after the end of the war—this at a time when most other WWI types had been considered obsolete at the end of that conflict in 1918.

Two F.2bs were gifted to New Zealand after the war, and these along with five others purchased subsequently went on to serve with the New Zealand Permanent Air Force. These were used in a number of roles, from training, joyrides, meteorological flights, army cooperation, aerial

surveying and photography. Three of these aircraft were written off in accidents.

In 1934 the NZPAF was renamed the Royal New Zealand Air Force, with the four surviving Bristol Fighters remaining in service until 1936—New Zealand being the last Commonwealth country to retire their F.2bs.

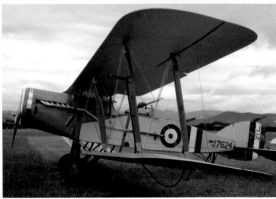

Year: 1917 *Built:* 5329 *Top Speed:* 198 km/h *Operational Ceiling:* 5500m *Wingspan:* 11.96m *Height:* 2.97m *Length:* 7.87m *Max Weight:* 1261kg *Engine:* 275hp Rolls Royce Falcon III *Climb:* 4.5m/s *Range:* 593km *Endurance:* 180mins *Armament:* 1 x .303 Vickers and 1 or 2 x Lewis in rear + up to 110kg bombs *This Aircraft:* Replica with 200hp Ranger engine, built in USA. *ZK-JNU*

Facing Page Pilot: Tim Sullivan

Fokker Dr.1 'Triplane'

152 / 17 Manfred von Richthofen

One of the most famous fighter aces of all time, Baron Manfred von Richthofen, like many of his contemporaries served in a cavalry unit before he transferred to the Imperial German Army Air Service (Luftstreitkräfte) in May 1915.

Initially serving as an observer in reconnaissance aircraft he entered pilot training in late 1915. By March 1916 he was back in the air piloting two-seater aircraft, and by September he had joined Jasta 2 as a fighter pilot. He scored his first confirmed victory over Cambrai in France on the 17th of September 1916.

After only a month in the air he had achieved 'Ace' status with six victories against Allied aircraft. As his reputation grew he began painting the fuselage of his aircraft (at the time an Albatros D.III) bright red, and became known to the British as the 'Red Baron'.

Fokker Dr.1 152/17 was only partially red and was flown by von Richthofen as a reserve aircraft. He scored his 64th, 65th and 66th victories while flying this aircraft.

Year: 1917   *Built:* 320   *Top Speed:* 185km/h   *Operational Ceiling:* 6100m   *Wingspan:* 7.19m   *Height:* 2.95m   *Length:* 5.77m
Max Weight: 586kg   *Engine:* 110hp Le Rhône rotary   *Climb:* 5.7m/s   *Range:* 300km   *Armament:* 2 x 7.92mm Spandau LMG
This Aircraft: Replica with a 220hp Continental radial engine, built in NZ in 1985 by Stuart Tantrum and John Lanham. ZK-FOK

Facing Page Pilot: John Lanham

Fokker Dr.1 'Triplane'

586 / 17 Lt. Hans Kirschstein

Kirschstein began the war as a Sapper, and served in Poland, Galacia and the Western Front until May 1917 when he transferred to the air service.

He initially flew two-seaters (and flew a bombing raid on Dover), but in March 1918 he joined Jasta 6 as a fighter pilot. By the end of May he'd scored 16 victories, and by June 24th had increased his score to 27.

The diagonal stripes on the aircraft were designed to put attacking pilots off their aim. The idea being that enemy pilots would sight along the lines, thinking they ran parallel with the wings and fuselage and this would cause them to aim in the wrong place. Kirschstein called his aircraft 'the optical illusion'.

Kirschstein was once rebuked by Manfred von Richthofen after downing two enemy aircraft. Richthofen did not tolerate his pilots allowing themselves to be shot and after discovering a bullet hole in the tail of Kirschstein's aircraft he is reported to have said:

"Your kills were respectable, but they mustn't be bought by shots in the back! Obviously you were lucky ....Any decent flyer would have clearly laid you flat... "

After Kirschstein's death in a flying accident in July 1918, 586/17 was flown by Ernst Udet, who with a score of 62 victories was the second highest scoring German ace after Manfred von Richthofen.

Year: 1917 Built: 320 Top Speed: 185km/h Operational Ceiling: 6100m Wingspan: 7.19m Height: 2.95m Length: 5.77m
Max Weight: 586kg Engine: 110hp Oberursel UR.II rotary Climb: 5.7m/s Range: 300km Armament: 2 x 7.92mm Spandau LMG
This Aircraft: Replica with a 165hp 7-cylinder air cooled Warner Scarab radial engine, built in the USA. ZK-JOC

Facing Page Pilot: Pete Cochrane

Fokker Dr.1 'Triplane'

Serial Unknown. Lt. Hans Müller

Like many others, Hans Müller initially served in the German Army, but then transferred to the Air Service in 1916. He flew two-seater aircraft until the end of 1917, when he transferred to single-seat fighters, and began to accumulate his final score of 12 victories.

In March 1918 he was shot down over No Man's Land, but managed to make it back to the German lines after force landing his aircraft.

On the morning of the 14th September 1918, he shot down three Spad XIIIs within a space of 15 minutes, and then later the same day claimed a fourth Spad from the same squadron.

Prior to April 1918 the 'national' markings painted on the tail, wings and fuselage of German aircraft often varied from unit to unit (as seen in the photographs below). The Dr.1s were initially finished with the Prussian 'Eiserne Kreuz' (Iron Cross), but some were later changed in the field to the 'Balkenkreuz' (Balkan Cross), for example Hans Kirschstein's aircraft.

In April 1918 an order was issued for all German aircraft to be repainted to use the Balkenkreuz as the national marking, hence all late war aircraft carried the straight-sided cross only.

Year: 1917 *Built:* 320 *Top Speed:* 185km/h *Operational Ceiling:* 6100m *Wingspan:* 7.19m *Height:* 2.95m *Length:* 5.77m
Max Weight: 586kg *Engine:* 110hp Oberursel UR.II rotary *Climb:* 5.7m/s *Range:* 300km *Armament:* 2 x 7.92mm Spandau LMG
This Aircraft: Replica with a 165hp 7-cylinder air cooled Warner Scarab radial engine, built in the USA. ZK-JOK

Facing Page Pilot: Jim Rankin

Fokker Dr.1 'Triplane'

521 / 17 Oblt. Robert Greim

The son of a Bavarian policeman, Greim had been an army cadet before the war and after serving with an artillery unit in the early part of the conflict, transferred to the Air Service in August 1915.

Initially flying two seaters he later joined Jasta 34b flying fighters and by the spring of 1918 he had over a dozen victories to his name (toward his final tally of 28).

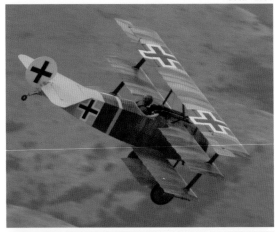

He flew this Dr.1 for a period in 1918, after Jasta 34b had been equipped with cast-off's from Jagdgeschwader I. Despite being second hand the aircraft were warmly received as they were superior to the older Albatros and Pfalz fighters the unit had been previously equipped with.

In June 1918 Greim had an encounter with a Bristol Fighter F.2b and his aircraft lost its cowling. This struck and damaged his top wing, along with the lower left interplane strut, but he managed to land the machine successfully.

Year: 1917   Built: 320   Top Speed: 185km/h   Operational Ceiling: 6100m   Wingspan: 7.19m   Height: 2.95m   Length: 5.77m
Max Weight: 586kg   Engine: 110hp Oberursel UR.II rotary   Climb: 5.7m/s   Range: 300km   Armament: 2 x 7.92mm Spandau LMG
This Aircraft: Replica with a 165hp 7-cylinder air cooled Warner Scarab radial engine, built in the USA.   ZK-JOB

Facing Page Pilot: Gavin Trethewy

Fokker Dr.1 'Triplane'

213 / 17 Lt. Friedrich (Fritz) Kempf

Written on the upper wing of this Dr.1 is Kempf's surname in large letters, while the mid-wing of has the legend 'kennscht mi noch?'

When translated this means roughly "Do you remember me?", and many commentators have speculated that it was designed to taunt the enemy into a dogfight. Others have noted that this phrase was merely a favourite saying of Kempf's with which he often greeted friends.

The aircraft as shown here is Kempf's Dr.1 in early 1918. By late April the Eiserne Kruz national markings had been replaced with the new thick style Balkenkruez. Kempf survived the war and ended with a final score of four victories.

Year: 1917 *Built:* 320 *Top Speed:* 185km/h *Operational Ceiling:* 6100m *Wingspan:* 7.19m *Height:* 2.95m *Length:* 5.77m
Max Weight: 586kg *Engine:* 110hp Oberursel UR.II rotary *Climb:* 5.7m/s *Range:* 300km *Armament:* 2 x 7.92mm Spandau LMG
This Aircraft: Replica with a 165hp 7-cylinder air cooled Warner Scarab radial engine, built in the USA. ZK-JOG

Facing Page Pilot: Greg MacDonald

Avro 504k

D-8781

Designed in 1913 by Alliot Verdon-Roe (founder of the A.V. Roe aircraft company), the 504 was one of the Royal Flying Corps primary service aircraft in the early stages of the First World War.

The Avro 504 was the first aircraft (type) to be used to strafe troops on the ground, and it also has the dubious honour of being the first British aircraft to have been shot down by enemy ground fire.

In November 1914 the Royal Naval Air Service used the type to conduct the first long-range bombing mission. Three 504s, each carrying four 20lb bombs attacked the Zeppelin factory at Freidrickshaven on the shores of Lake Constance in Germany.

While the type flew well, new aircraft soon replaced the 504 in combat, and it was subsequently relegated to the role of standard trainer for the rest of the war.

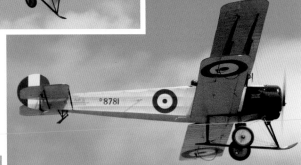

In 1920 Britain gave New Zealand twenty 504s as part of the Imperial Gift program. A further six were purchased over the next few years.

Year: 1913   *Built:* 8970   *Top Speed:* 145km/h   *Operational Ceiling:* 4875m   *Wingspan:* 10.97m   *Height:* 3.17m   *Length:* 8.97m
Max Weight: 830kg   *Engine:* 110-130hp Clerget rotary   *Climb:* 3.6m/s   *Range:* 402km   *Endurance:* 165mins   *Armament:* Unarmed
but provision for four 9kg bombs   *This Aircraft:* Replica with a 145hp Warner Scarab radial engine, built in the UK.   ZK-EHB

Facing Page Pilot: Gavin Trethewey

Nieuport 24

N1895A - Lt Charles Nungesser

Developed in 1917, the N.24 was Nieuport's attempt to prolong the success of its line of sesquiplane aircraft, which had begun with the Nieuport 11 and had progressed through to the Nieuport 17.

The lower wing of these types was only half the width of the top wing (hence sesquiplane), and was staggered so there was little (airflow) interference between the two wings. The result of this arrangement was the 'V' struts between the wings which was characteristic of many of the Nieuport designs. The N.24 model was the first Nieuport aircraft to feature a circular fuselage cross-section, as opposed to the slab-sided fuselages of earlier models.

While the Nieuport 17 had been a highly successful fighter, flown by aces such as Albert Ball, Billy Bishop, Charles Nungesser and Georges Guynemer, the N.24 did not have the same degree of success. The Royal Naval Air Service used fifty British-built N.24s operationally, but France's *Aéronautique Militaire* only used the type in a training role. Likewise the 261 aircraft purchased by the American Expeditionary Force late in 1917 were only used as pursuit (fighter) trainers. By the time the N.24 was ready for deployment, many French units had already begun to re-equip with faster SPAD built aircraft.

The N.27, with slightly modified armament and undercarriage details, was the final development in the sesquiplane line of Nieuport aircraft. The later Nieuport 28 reverted to standard bi-plane configuration with upper and lower wings of the same depth.

Year: 1917 *Built:* 420+ *Top Speed:* 187km/h *Operational Ceiling:* 5550m *Wingspan:* 8.18m *Height:* 2.44m *Length:* 5.88m
Max Weight: 544kg *Engine:* 110hp Le Rhône rotary *Climb:* 3.8m/s *Endurance:* 90mins *Armament:* 1 x .303 synchronised
Vickers or 1 x .303 Lewis on upper wing *This Aircraft:* Replica with a 145hp Warner Scarab engine, built in the USA. ZK-JOZ

Facing Page Pilot: Keith Skilling

Pfalz D.III

'The Blue Max' colour scheme

The Pfalz D.III began to appear at the front in August 1917. Along with its main contemporaries, the Albatros (D.Va) and Fokker (D.VII), this was one of the types that helped improve the German Air Service's fortunes at a time when the Allies has been enjoying superiority in the air.

With a 175hp engine, the Pfalz was a heavier aircraft than the Fokker and Albatros types, and often lost height during combat with enemy aircraft. However, it was structurally very sound, and did not suffer some of the failures that others (such as the Albatros D.Vs) did. This integrity also helped to ensure the type was a successful diving fighter as it gained speed rapidly in a dive, and was used with considerable effect to attack and destroy Allied balloons.

This replica was one of two built for the 1966 motion picture 'The Blue Max', and is shown here in the inaccurate colour scheme it wore for that movie. German aircraft of the time were often covered with linen printed with a five-colour lozenge scheme, whereas this aircraft was painted in a spurious 'seven-colour' lozenge scheme for the movie. It is believed that the star of the movie, actor George Peppard, actually flew this aircraft on several occasions during filming of the motion picture.

Year: 1917   Built: 1010   Top Speed: 185 km/h   Operational Ceiling: 5200m   Wingspan: 9.4m   Height: 2.67m   Length: 6.95m   Max Weight: 935kg   Engine: 175hp Mercedes D.III water cooled inline   Climb: 2.33 m/s   Endurance: 150 mins   Armament: 2 x 7.92mm Spandau LMG   This Aircraft: Replica with a 145hp 4-cylinder Gypsy Major, built in the UK (was N905AC)   [OAHC]   ZK-JPI

Fokker D.IV

Generic colour scheme

From late 1915 to early 1916, the German Army Air Service held a significant advantage over the Allies with its Fokker E.III Eindecker monoplane. However by the summer of 1916, the E.III was becoming outdated and surpassed by more advanced Allied fighters of the time.

To counter the Allied threat, Fokker developed the 120hp engined D.I biplane, but it proved to be a mediocre aircraft and only a small number were built.

In an effort to improve the design, Fokker re-equipped the aircraft with a 160hp engine, slightly modified the aircraft, and released it as the D.IV. While this provided a performance boost, the aircraft still did not have the maneuverability desired of a fighter, and as the newer Albatros D.II and D.III fighters became available, the Fokker D.I/IVs were eventually relegated to training duties.

This aircraft has not been displayed at a New Zealand airshow, though from time to time has been seen standing at rest next to some of its Fokker brethren at Omaka and Hood Aerodromes.

Year: 1916 *Built:* 44 *Top Speed:* 160km/h *Operational Ceiling:* 4000m *Wingspan:* 9.7m *Height:* 2.75m *Length:* 6.3m
Max Weight: 840kg *Engine:* 160hp Mercedes D.III inline straight-6 *Climb:* 5.6m/s *Range:* 220km *Armament:* 2 x 7.92mm
Spandau LMG 08/15 machine guns *This Aircraft:* Replica with a 150hp CASA Tigre engine. Built in the USA. ZK-JPV

Halberstadt D.IV

Generic 1916 Halberstadt colour scheme

The Halberstadt D.I/II was one of the first biplane fighters deployed by Germany in 1916, and it was introduced at the time when the Fokker E.III Eindecker monoplanes had begun to lose their effectiveness.

From March through September that year, 146 examples of the single gun D.I/II/III models were produced. While they enjoyed a brief period of superiority over the Allies, with their 120hp engines they were under-powered. As numbers of the better performing Albatros fighters became available, the Halberstadts' were withdrawn and relegated to a training role.

With a larger 150hp engine and twin machine guns, the new D.IV was designed to compete with the Albatros fighters. This was not a success and only three models of this variant were built. An early 1917 report notes:

... in keeping earlier elements within the design, the D.IV has fallen behind the times and can no longer compete with the others that have advanced past this technology.....

A further 57 D.V aircraft were built which reverted to the earlier 120hp Argus engine, though other refinements including improved streamlining ensured it did perform better than the earlier models.

Year: 1916   Built: 3   Top Speed: 145km/h*   Operational Ceiling: 5550m   Wingspan: 8.8m   Height: 2.67m   Length: 7.3m   Max Weight: approx 730kg   Engine: 150hp Benz B.III inline engine   Endurance: 90mins   Armament: 1 x 7.92mm Spandau LMG
This Aircraft: Replica with a 150hp CASA Tigre engine, built in the USA.   (* Performance stats for D.II)   [OAHC]   ZK-JOW

Facing Page Pilot: Dave Horrell

Airco DH.2

7855 - 24 Sqn, Royal Flying Corps

The DH.2 was designed by Geoffrey de Havilland as a single seat fighting scout to replace the larger two-seat DH.1.

Although he had already designed the B.E.2, a conventional tractor biplane, de Havilland reverted to the more primitive looking pusher configuration for the DH.1 and DH.2 because at the time Great Britain did not have a reliable interrupter mechanism to allow machine gun fire through rotating propellers.

The Lewis gun was originally attached with a flexible mount to allow it to be aimed to the left or right, but many pilots found this inadequate. The gun was subsequently firmly mounted to the forward fuselage instead, allowing the pilot to aim the aircraft and not the gun. This quickly showed the DH.2 to be a capable fighter despite its most serious opposition during the first half of 1916 being the modern looking Fokker E.III 'Eindecker.'

DH.2s served on the front line in France throughout 1916, but by March 1917 were being withdrawn from service. The survivors were allocated to training units for the remainder of the war.

Year: 1915 *Built:* 453 *Top Speed:* 149 km/h *Operational Ceiling:* 4420m *Wingspan:* 8.61m *Height:* 2.91m *Length:* 7.68m
Max Weight: 654kg *Engine:* 100hp Gnome Monosoupape rotary *Climb:* 2.76m/s *Range:* 400km *Endurance:* 165 mins
Armament: 1 x .303 Lewis gun *This Aircraft:* Replica with 125hp Kinner radial engine, built in the USA (was N5496) *[OAHC]* ZK-JOJ

Facing Page Pilot: Simon Paul

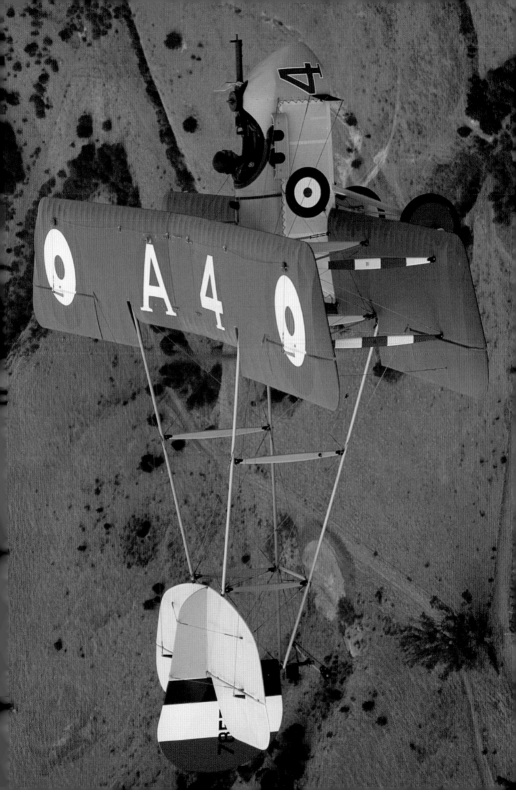

Airco DH.5

A9242 - No 2 Sqn Australian Flying Corps

Designed in 1916 when the DH.2 and F.E.8 'pusher' types were in widespread use, the DH.5 was Geoffrey de Havilland's attempt to create a fighter with the performance of a 'tractor' aircraft, but with the better visibility common to the older 'pushers'. The forward field of vision was significantly improved by positioning the upper wing toward the rear of the cockpit in a 'staggered' configuration.

This was also the first of the de Havilland designs to feature an inter-rupter mechanism to allow a machine gun to fire through the propeller arc.

Unfortunately the type did not per-form well at high altitudes. However its robustness, and the pilots field of view made the DH.5 well suited to ground attack duties,

even though with only a single Vickers machine gun the aircraft was somewhat under-armed for operations in 1917.

The original A9242 was a 'Presentation Aircraft' purchased for the Australian Flying Corps by public fund rasing efforts. The text on the side of the aircraft reads:

New South Wales No14 Battleplane
Subscribed & Collected By Women of
New South Wales

Year: 1917 *Built:* 552 *Top Speed:* 158 km/h *Operational Ceiling:* 4875m *Wingspan:* 7.82m *Height:* 2.78m *Length:* 6.71m
Max Weight: 677kg *Engine:* 110hp Le Rhône 9 J rotary *Endurance:* 165 mins *Armament:* 1 x .303 Vickers with provision for
two 11kg Cooper bombs *This Aircraft:* Replica with O-320 Lycoming engine, built in the USA *[OAHC]* ZK-JOQ

Facing Page Pilot: Stuart Tantrum

Nieuport 24

N2546 - 2nd Lt. Gilbert Discours

As a hussar (cavalryman) at the start of the war, Discours received a *Croix de Guerre* after an eventful night patrol action. In 1917, following the advice of an officer he asked to transfer to fly, and was accepted for pilot training. By September he had received his wings and by December he'd been assigned to the 87th air unit flying Nieuports and Spads. The white cat on the fuselage of the aircraft was the standard unit marking.

In February 1918 he shot down a German aircraft, followed by another in March. For this, he received a second *Croix de Guerre.*

In August 1918, he gained his third official victory, and in September he shot down his fourth and final enemy aircraft. He received his third *Croix de Guerre* in October with the citation:

"Excellent pilot, gifted with the greatest quality of agility and cold blooded courage".

In recognition of his service, he received a fourth *Croix de Guerre* in September 1919. He decided to remain in the French military, finally retiring as a Major in 1934, though he was later recalled for service during WW2.

Year: 1917   Built: 420+   Top Speed: 187km/h   Operational Ceiling: 5550m   Wingspan: 8.18m   Height: 2.44m   Length: 5.88m
Max Weight: 544kg   Engine: 110hp Le Rhône rotary   Climb: 3.8m/s   Endurance: 90mins   Armament: 1 x .303 synchronised Vickers or 1 x .303 Lewis on upper wing   This Aircraft: Replica with a 145hp Warner Scarab engine, built in the USA.   ZK-JOZ

Facing Page Pilot: Tim Sullivan

Bristol Fighter F.2b

B1112 - Capt. C. Jones, 16 Sqn, RFC

The F.2b was originally designed as a potential replacement for the Royal Aircraft Factory B.E.2 series of two seat observation and reconnaissance aircraft.

The type first entered service in April 1917 but its introduction did not go well as the pilots had been warned to avoid violent maneuvers during combat, and to fly the aircraft like standard two-seaters. This resulted in many F.2bs being shot down and the type was almost withdrawn from service immediately. However, as the F.2b crews became more experienced on the type, and adopted combat tactics more usual of single seaters, it was found to be a very capable and successful fighter.

Sir Keith Park, a New Zealander (famous for his command of Number 11 Fighter Group in south-east England during the Battle of Britain in 1940), flew Bristol Fighters with the Royal Flying Corps from July 1917.

By the end of the war he had accumulated a score of twenty victories, and had been shot down once by anti-aircraft fire, and once by German aircraft.

It is believed that the first aircraft to touch down on the historic Omaka Aerodrome (Blenheim, NZ) were two Bristol F.2bs of the New Zealand Permanent Air Force.

Year: 1917 *Built:* 5329 *Top Speed:* 198 km/h *Operational Ceiling:* 5500m *Wingspan:* 11.96m *Height:* 2.97m *Length:* 7.87m
Max Weight: 1261kg *Engine:* 275hp Rolls Royce Falcon III v12 *Climb:* 4.5m/s *Range:* 593km *Endurance:* 180mins *Armament:*
1 x .303 Vickers and 1 or 2 x Lewis in rear + up to 110kg bombs *This Aircraft:* Replica with 200hp Ranger engine. ZK-JNU

Facing Page Pilot: Tim Sullivan

Etrich (a.k.a. Rumpler) Taube

Initially designed by Austrian Igor Etrich in 1909 the Taube ("dove") was the first massed produced aircraft in Germany, and was used extensively by that country, Italy and Austria-Hungary in the years leading up to the First World War. Known as a very stable aircraft it was well suited for use as an observation and reconnaissance aircraft, and the translucent nature of its wings often made it difficult to see from the ground if it was flying at any significant altitude.

Though named after a bird, the aircraft's unusually shaped wings were in fact modelled on a 'flying' tree seed, similar to that of a sycamore. The large wing area, combined with the irregular shape of the wing, and the fact that the aircraft was designed before the advent of ailerons for control meant that the aircraft features a veritable spiders-web of control cables. These cables help to achieve the necessary 'wing-warping' required for lateral control during flight (like curling the back of a paper aeroplane to make it

fly in one direction or another).

Etrich licenced the aircraft to be built by Lohner in Austria and by Rumpler in Germany. Rumpler subsequently stopped paying royalties on each aircraft built, and after a dispute, Etrich eventually gave up his patent rights. This lack of a licence fee then saw over a dozen companies start to build the aircraft, including many who would go on to be major aircraft producers during the war. In addition to Rumpler, companies such as Albatros, Aviatik, Gotha, Halberstadt, Roland all produced Taube variants and used the aircraft to gain experience with the process of mass producing aircraft.

By the time war broke out in July 1914 more modern designs had already begun to appear,

and the Taube was soon superceded. However in the early months of the war the type played a significant part in military operations. Taube aircraft were used very successfully by the Germans during the Battle of Tannenberg on the Eastern Front to observe and monitor the advance of the Russian army.

Currently on display in the OAHC, this replica aircraft was built in Germany as an airworthy example. The photos below show the aircraft being displayed in Berlin in 2004 before it joined the collection in New Zealand.

Year: 1912 *Built:* approx 500 *Top Speed:* 115 km/h *Operational Ceiling:* 3000m *Wingspan:* 14.35m *Height:* 3.15m *Length:* 9.85m
Max Weight: 870kg *Engine:* 70 to 120hp Mercedes or Argus inline *Endurance:* up to 240 mins *Armament:* Handheld firearms
This Aircraft: Airworthy Replica with a 105hp Walter Minor engine, built in Germany. Not flown in NZ, static display only *[OAHC]*

Morane-Saulnier BB/BH

No 60 Sqn, RFC

Morane-Saulnier built their first aircraft in 1911, a monoplane dubbed the Model A, which won the Paris to Madrid air race that year. Over the course of the next few years the company continued to produced a string of monoplanes at a time when other aircraft producers were concentrating on multi-wing designs.

During the early part of the war these monoplane designs reached a zenith in the Type L and P parasol monoplanes (with the wing suspended above the fuselage), of which nearly 600 of each were built. While the bulk of these were used by the French *Aviation Militaire*, a considerable number were also operated by the Royal Flying Corps (RFC) and Royal Naval Air Service (RNAS).

Later in the war the parasol monoplane Type AI was built in considerable numbers (over 1200). However the type was quickly superceded by new Spad-built biplane fighters and only had a short operational career (a couple of months in early 1918), after which it was relegated to a training role.

In March 1915 a Morane-Saulnier Type L was the first aircraft to be fitted with a forward-facing machine gun firing through the propeller arc. Frenchman Roland Garros equipped his aircraft with a Hotchkiss machine gun and attached two deflector plates to the blades of his propeller. The idea being that any stray bullets that might otherwise hit his own propeller as it turned in front of the gun would be simply deflected away by the steel plate and therefore would not cause any damage.

Garros had immediate success with his modified Type L and shot down five enemy aircraft in the first few weeks of April. At this stage of the war most aerial combat was still being fought with small arms fire, or by gunners in two seat aircraft—it came as a complete surprise to the German pilots that Garros attacked that they were being shot at by an aircraft with a forward firing machine gun.

Unfortunately the Frenchman was shot down and force landed behind enemy lines on the 19th April 1915 and his aircraft was captured before it was completely destroyed. The Germans examined the aircraft and soon discovered the secret of his success and then undertook to improve the design. By late 1915 the engineers at Fokker had developed a successful interrupter mechanism (thereby negating the need for steel plate deflectors on the propeller blades) and this was soon fitted to the Fokker E.I/III Eindecker, with enormous success.

Built specially to an order for a reconnaissance aircraft for the RFC, the Type BB was a conventional two-seat biplane design based on the fuselage of the Type P. Designed to have a 100hp Le Rhône engine, shortages of these engines meant that most of the aircraft of the type used 80hp engines instead. These aircraft were fitted with a large spinner over the two blade propeller (as seen on this aircraft) and some sources indicate these were designated as the Type BH. No. 60 Sqn RFC and No.4 Sqn RNAS both used the Type BH while deployed in France from mid-late 1916. A number of the 60 Squadron aircraft were fitted with a second machine gun mounted on the top wing, and were used as fighters.

Late production models were fitted with a 110hp engine and these Type BBs were operated by No.1 and No. 3 Sqns RFC.

Year: 1915 Built: 94 Top Speed: 147 km/h Operational Ceiling: 4000m Wingspan: 8.65m Height: 2.54m Length: 7.0m
Max Weight: 750kg Engine: 80/110hp Le Rhône rotary Endurance: ca 160mins Armament: 1 x .303 Lewis for observer and in some cases an extra 1 x .303 Lewis mounted on top wing This Aircraft: Replica, built to airworthy standard in USA. [OAHC]

Fokker E.III 'Eindecker'

105/17 - Vfw. Ernst Udet, Jasta 15

Designed by Dutch engineer Anthony Fokker in early 1915, the E.I 'Eindecker' monoplane was the first purpose built German fighter aircraft, and was closely modelled on the pre-war Morane-SaulnierType H. German company Pfalz Flugzeugwerke produced around 100 variants of the Type H aircraft under licence, and these were known as the Pfalz E.I through E.VI.

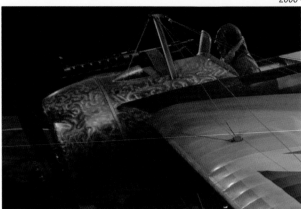

Equipped with a new machine gun interrupter mechanism designed by Fokker himself (after he had examined the deflector plate equipped Morane-Saulnier Type L of Roland Garros), the aircraft was the first fighter to feature a forward facing machine gun that would fire through the propeller arc without hitting the blades.

The Fokker E.I began appearing in numbers at the front in mid-1916, usually as a single aircraft attached to each *Feldflieger Abteilung* ('Field Flying Company').These fighter aircraft acted as armed escorts to the normally unarmed two seat reconnaissance aircraft in each unit.

Lt. Kurt Wintgens scored the first Eindecker victory in July 1915 when he shot down a two seat Morane-Saulnier L. By October 1915 the type had become a dominate force on the Western Front reigning almost totally unopposed by the Allies through until early 1916. The success of the type during this period lead to the description of the 'Fokker Scourge', and one aircraft type in particular, the luckless Royal Aircraft Factory B.E.2c quickly earned the nickname 'Fokker Fodder'.

By early 1916 the Eindeckers began to encounter the more capable Airco DH.2, Nieuport N.11, and Morane-Saulnier Type N aircraft and the 'scourge' was

effectively countered. By summer 1916 most Eindeckers had been withdrawn from front line service on the Western Front, but they continued to serve on the Eastern Front until the end of 1916.A number of the aircraft were also used in Mesopotamia, Palestine and Turkey.

A number of German aces began their fighting career in the Eindecker. Oswald Boelcke, a master tactician (and considered the father of the German fighter forces), scored 19 of his total of 40 victories while flying Eindeckers. Max Immelman achieved 15 victories before he was killed in June 1916 when his E.III broke up in flight. Before his death Immelman had experimented with fitting three machine guns to a Fokker E.IV (a new higher powered model designed to

carry two guns), but the guns jammed often and the configuration was never used again.

Ernst Udet, with a total of 62 victories, was the second highest scoring German ace behind Manfred von Richthofen, and he also used the E.III with considerable skill between March 1916 and January 1917.

One original example of the E.III (201/16) still survives and is on display in the Science Museum in London. The aircraft was captured intact by the British when the novice pilot of the aircraft became disoriented while flying in hazy conditions, and mistakenly landed at the British airfield at St Omer.The hapless German was forced to surrender before he realised his mistake and could destroy the aircraft.

Year: 1915 Built: approx 416 (all variants) Top Speed: 133 km/h Operational Ceiling: 3500m Wingspan: 9.52m Height: 2.79m
Length: 7.3m Max Weight: 610kg Engine: 100hp Oberursel Ur.1 rotary engine Endurance: 165 mins Armament: 1 x 7.92mm
Parabellum MG14 machine gun, E.IV model featured 2 x 7.92mm MG This Aircraft: New TVAL reproduction (static) [OAHC]

Albatros B.II

The B.II was the first mass produced type built by Albatros Flugzeugwerke. The aircraft was identical to the earlier B.I model designed by Ernst Heinkel in 1913, with the exception that it had a shorter wingspan.

As with all the 'B' class aircraft used by Germany, the Albatros B.II was an unarmed aircraft, used extensively for observation, reconnaissance, and minor tactical bombing roles in the early part of the war. By the time the armed 'C' class two seaters began to arrive in the summer of 1915, the B.II was essentially obsolete. However its excellent flying characteristics made it ideal for training, and it undertook that role until the end of the war.

Like its early war British counterpart the B.E.2c, the pilot of the Albatros B.II flew the aircraft from the rear cockpit. This meant that the observer (often armed with a hand held firearm) was seated in the front cockpit between the two wings and amongst the struts and rigging. This seating arrangement was found to be generally unsatisfactory in practice but it was not until the 'C' class aircraft were developed that this seating arrangement was reversed so that the observer/gunner would have a better field of view and field of fire from the rear cockpit.

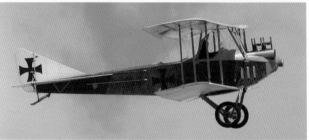

After the outbreak of the war an example of the B.II was interned in (neutral) Sweden where it was later copied and manufactured by five different companies. The type was still being used as a trainer in Sweden until as late as 1935.

Like the Taube in the OAHC, this B.II replica was built in Germany as an airworthy example. Two of the photos at right show the aircraft being displayed in Germany before it joined the New Zealand collection in 2006.

Year: 1914 *Built:* 1360 *Top Speed:* 105 km/h *Operational Ceiling:* 3000m *Wingspan:* 12.8m *Height:* 3.15m *Length:* 7.63m
Max Weight: 1070kg *Engine:* 100hp Mercedes D.I 6-cylinder water-cooled inline *Endurance:* 240 mins *Armament:* None.
Observers with hand held firearms. *This Aircraft:* Replica with a 165hp Walter Minor VI engine, built in Germany. *[OAHC]*

Royal Aircraft Factory R.E.8

A4397 'D' - Capt. R.G. Francis

The Royal Aircraft Factory's "Reconnaissance Experimental 8" was designed as a replacement for the earlier B.E.2 series. With a more powerful engine and better armament (including a synchronised forward firing machine gun on the left of the fuselage) the R.E.8 was used in large numbers until the end of the war in November 1918. Only two original examples survive—this static reproduction was built by TVAL in 2006 and was displayed in the OAHC for several years.

Nicknamed the 'Harry Tate' after a music hall entertainer of the time, the R.E.8 was the most widely used British two-seater aircraft on the Western Front. The type also saw significant service in Italy,

Mesopotamia and Palestine. Despite being outclassed by most enemy fighters, the R.E.8 was engaged in all manner of operations from observation duties, pure reconnaissance, night bombing and general ground attack. The colour scheme of this air-

craft representzs that of A4397 which was flown by No. 3 Sqn Australian Flying Corps. With pilot Capt R.G. Francis at the controls the aircraft set a remarkable service record on the Western Front by flying a total of over 440 operational hours during 147 separate sorties across the front lines.

Year: 1916 Built: 4099 Top Speed: 164 km/h Operational Ceiling: 4115m Wingspan: 12.98m Height: 3.49m Length: 8.5m
Max Weight: 1301kg Engine: 150hp R.A.F.4a air cooled v-12 inline Endurance: 255 mins Armament: 1 x .303 Vickers forward facing, 1 or 2 x .303 Lewis in rear cockpit, plus up to 102kg of bombs This Aircraft: New TVAL reproduction (static)

Royal Aircraft Factory S.E.5a

D6864 - Capt K. L. Caldwell

Along with the Royal Aircraft Factory R.E.8, this reproduction aircraft was one of the first new-build aircraft to be constructed by The Vintage Aviator Ltd. Built using authentic construction methods and materials, the building of this S.E.5a allowed the TVAL craftsmen to hone their skills before beginning work on the three airworthy examples of the S.E.5a that were subsequently built. While this aircraft is not airworthy, it is never-the-less one of the most accurate and authentic S.E.5s built in the last ninety years.

Captain Keith 'Grid' Caldwell was New Zealand's top scoring ace during the First World War. Born in Wellington and educated in Wanganui and Auckland, Caldwell was one of the first two pupils at the Walsh Brothers New Zealand Flying School in Auckland. He passed his flight tests in December 1915 and by April 1916 he was in the UK and had received his commission with the Royal Flying Corps.

Posted to France with No. 8 Sqn RFC in July 1916 he scored his first victory in September that year (a Roland C.II) while flying an R.A.F. B.E.2d—a slow and almost obsolete two seater. In November he was posted to No. 60 Sqn to fly single-seat Nieuport fighters and over the course of the next eight months scored another seven victories—a single Albatros C and six Albatros D.IIIs. No 60 Sqn converted to R.A.F. S.E.5a's in July 1917 and Caldwell scored his last victory with the unit by shooting down another Albatros C in September.

In September 1917 he received the Military Cross "... for conspicuous gallantry and devotion to duty when leading offensive patrols...", and then in October he was recalled to England where he spent the next six months as an instructor. Promoted to Major he was sent back to France in April 1918 to take command of the S.E.5a-equipped No. 74 Squadron—a position he held until the end of the war. In the seven months leading up to the Armistice in November 1918 he increased his tally to 25, which included five Pfalz D.III scouts and nine Fokker D.VIIs. At least four of these victories were scored while he was flying D6864.

The exhibit in the Omaka Aviation Heritage Centre (shown here) illustrates an event while Caldwell was with 74 Sqn. His aircraft had been damaged in a mid-air collision and he was having difficulty controlling the aircraft.

Preparing to jump from the aircraft he climbed out onto the wing and found that his unbalanced weight made the aircraft more controllable. In this attitude he 'flew' his S.E.5a down to near ground level, jumping clear of the aircraft just a few feet from the ground—miraculously walking away from the incident.

Year: 1917 *Built:* 5205 *Top Speed:* 193 km/h *Operational Ceiling:* 5944m *Wingspan:* 8.11m *Height:* 2.89m *Length:* 6.38m *Max Weight:* 902kg *Engine:* 200hp Wolesley Viper water cooled V12 *Range:* 483km *Endurance:* 180 mins *Armament:* 1 x .303 Vickers + 1 x .303 Lewis on upper wing, up to 4 x 11kg bombs. *This Aircraft:* New TVAL reproduction (static only) *[OAHC]*.

Siemens-Schuckert D.IV

Generic colour scheme

In 1916 Siemens-Schuckert produced the D.I, their first biplane fighter which was essentially a direct copy of the French Nieuport 11. Only 95 of these aircraft were produced and few saw combat service as by the time the required 100hp Siemens-Halske Sh.1 rotary engines became available in numbers the aircraft design had almost become obsolete.

Siemens-Halske reworked the engine and produced a more powerful 11-cylinder 160hp version, the Sh.III. When this new engine was married to a D.I airframe, the resulting aircraft was dubbed the Siemens-Schuckert D.III. This new aircraft displayed a remarkable rate of climb and many of Jagdgeschwader II's pilots were very enthusiastic about the new aircraft when approximately 40 of them were delivered to front line units in March 1918. A total of 80 D.IIIs were built before the improved D.IV model became available in August 1918.

Featuring narrower wings and sporting the newer 200hp Sh.III engines, the D.IV quickly proved that it was superior to any other fighter in use by either the Germans or Allies at that time. Unfortunately by the time the war ended only 120 D.IVs had been built, and only about half of those had been delivered to front line combat units. Like many of Germany's advanced aircraft designs late in the Second World War, the D.IV proved to be too little, too late to make much of an impact during the First World War. Production of the D.IV contin-

ued after the Armistice until mid-1919, and many examples of the aircraft were supplied to Switzerland who operated the type well into the 1920s.

The aircraft on display at the Omaka Aviation Heritage Centre was built in the USA as an airworthy example and did fly on a number of occasions with the Frank Ryder Collection. However since joining the 1914-1918 Aviation Heritage Trust collection in New Zealand the aircraft has not flown. and will likely remain as a 'snow-bound' static display aircraft.

Year: 1918 Built: approx 150 Top Speed: 190 km/h Operational Ceiling: 8000m Wingspan: 8.35m Height: 2.72m Length: 5.7m Max Weight: 735kg Engine: 160/200hp Siemens-Halske Sh.III 11-cylinder geared rotary Climb: 6.45m/s Endurance: 120 mins Armament: 2 x 7.92mm Spandau This Aircraft: Replica, originally with a 185 hp Warner Super Scarab, built in the USA. [OAHC]

Nieuport 24

N1895A - Lt Charles Nungesser

With 45 official victories by the end of the war, Charles Nungesser was France's third highest ranking ace of the war behind René Fonck (75) and Georges Guynemer (53).

Initially fighting with the French Army as a cavalryman, he was wounded on several occasions, and was eventually invalided out of that service.

After joining the French *Aviation Militaire* he continued to be determined to fight for his country and was seriously wounded on several more occasions, which doubtless affected his ability to increase his tally.

In May 1927 Nungesser and Francois Coli attempted a trans-Atlantic flight from France to North America, flying *L'Oiseau Blanc* (The White Bird), a Levasseur L.9 biplane. The pair were last sighted over Ireland, but subsequently went missing, presumed dead.

As with ZK-JOZ, the N.24 that was first displayed in Nungesser's 'Knight Of Death' colours, the scheme on this aircraft is not accurate as there is no record of the ace having flown an N.24. The scheme is that worn by Nungesser's earlier Nieuport 17.

Year: 1917 *Built:* 420+ *Top Speed:* 187km/h *Operational Ceiling:* 5550m *Wingspan:* 8.18m *Height:* 2.44m *Length:* 5.88m *Max Weight:* 544kg *Engine:* 110hp Le Rhône rotary *Climb:* 3.8m/s *Endurance:* 90mins *Armament:* 1 x .303 synchronised Vickers or 1 x .303 Lewis on upper wing *This Aircraft:* Replica with a 165hp Warner Scarab engine, built in USA *[OAHC]* ZK-NIE

Facing Page Pilot: John Lanham

Fokker Dr.1 'Triplane'

425 / 17 Manfred von Richthofen

In January 1917 von Richthofen became the commanding officer of Jasta 11 and by June 1917 he was commanding Jagdgeschwader 1, a combined force of four individual Jasta (fighter squadrons).

Only twenty of von Richthofen's total of 80 victories were scored while flying the Fokker Dr.1. Between late 1916 and his death in April 1918 he flew a variety of fighter aircraft, including Albatros D.II and D.III's, a Halberstadt D.II and an Albatros D.V. Early in 1918 von Richthofen helped with the development of the Fokker D.VII but he never had the chance to fly that aircraft in combat.

While pursuing an Allied aircraft on 21 April 1918, von Richthofen was shot down and killed. While Canadian Sopwith Camel pilot Arthur Brown was officially credited with the 'kill', other evidence suggests that Richthofen may have been killed by a single shot fired from Australian ground troops.

Initially buried in France with full military honours (by the Allies), Richthofen's body was later exhumed and reburied in the family cemetery at Wiesbaden in Germany.

Year: 1917 *Built:* 320 *Top Speed:* 185km/h *Operational Ceiling:* 6100m *Wingspan:* 7.19m *Height:* 2.95m *Length:* 5.77m
Max Weight: 586kg *Engine:* 110hp Oberursel UR.II rotary *Climb:* 5.7m/s *Range:* 300km *Armament:* 2 x 7.92mm Spandau LMG
This Aircraft: Replica with a 220hp Continental radial engine built by Stuart Tantrum & John Lanham. *[OAHC]* ZK-FOK

Facing Page Pilot: Stuart Tantrum

Fokker Dr.1 'Triplane'

564/17 Lt Werner Steinhäuser

Jagdstaffel (Jasta) 11 was formed in September 1916 when the German Air Service decided to create a number of specialist fighter squadrons.

Steinhäuser joined Jasta 11 in November 1917. Having scored ten victories, he was killed in action while flying a Fokker D.VII a few days before his 22nd birthday in June 1918.

This aircraft was his second machine, which he was flying by April 1918—the first had a scheme similar to this, but with a red fuselage band and yellow crosses—it also featured the earlier *Eiserne Kruz* style German national markings. Both machines sported the standard Jasta 11 red cowl, wheel covers and struts.

Year: 1917   *Built:* 320   *Top Speed:* 185km/h   *Operational Ceiling:* 6100m   *Wingspan:* 7.19m   *Height:* 2.95m   *Length:* 5.77m
Max Weight: 586kg   *Engine:* 110hp Oberursel UR.II rotary   *Climb:* 5.7m/s   *Range:* 300km   *Armament:* 2 x 7.92mm Spandau LMG
This Aircraft: Replica with a 165hp 7-cylinder air cooled Warner Scarab radial engine, built in the USA. *[OAHC]*   ZK-JOC

Facing Page Pilot: Scott McKenzie

Fokker Dr.1 'Triplane'

545 / 17 Lt Hans Weiss

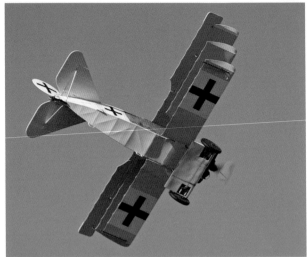

Serving as the CO of Jasta 11 from the 8th April 1918 until his death on 2nd May, Weiss was the unit's commander at the time of Manfred von Richthofen's death on the 21st April—it is recorded that von Richthofen and Weiss actually flew together earlier that day.

Some reports suggest that Weiss' Dr.1 was painted white all-over (in German *wiess* means white). However the colour was only applied to the top wing, tail, rear fuselage and the upper turtle deck.This colour distribution was common for formation leaders in Jagdgeschwader 1 and when viewed from above could cause the aircraft to appear solid white.

On May 2nd 1918 Weiss was shot down over Méricourt (and killed) by Canadian ace Lt Merril Taylor of 209 Sqn. Lt Taylor mentioned a "white triplane" in his combat report but other 209 Sqn pilots described the enemy formation as "red-nosed triplanes" (i.e. the common Jasta 11 adornment), so it's safe to assume the aircraft was Weiss' partially white aircraft.

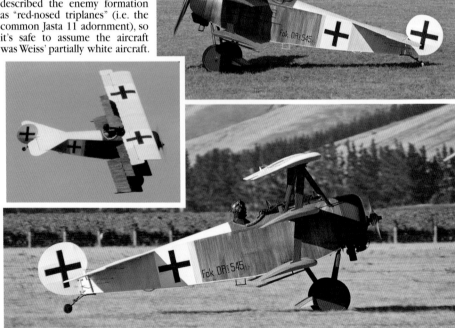

Year: 1917   Built: 320   Top Speed: 185km/h   Operational Ceiling: 6100m   Wingspan: 7.19m   Height: 2.95m   Length: 5.77m
Max Weight: 586kg   Engine: 110hp Oberursel UR.II rotary   Climb: 5.7m/s   Range: 300km   Armament: 2 x 7.92mm Spandau LMG
This Aircraft: Replica with a 165hp 7-cylinder air cooled Warner Scarab radial engine, built in the USA.   ZK-FOC

Facing Page Pilot: Frank Parker

Fokker Dr.1 'Triplane'

454 / 17 Oblt. Lothar von Richthofen

Like his older brother Manfred, Lothar was initially a cavalry officer when war broke out. He joined the Imperial German Army Air Service in 1915, and by March 1917 was assigned to Jasta 11, his brother's unit.

He was seriously wounded three times, held the position of Jasta 11 CO on four separate occasions, and scored a total of 40 victories. Unlike his brother, he survived the war, but was killed in an accident in 1922 when flying a commercial aircraft from Berlin to Hamburg.

Late in 2008 this aircraft was used in the filming of a short movie for the Australian War Memorial Museum. Additional spurious markings were added to the fuselage and tail colour scheme (*see the inset photo centre right*) in order to convert the aircraft into an 'anonymous' Dr.1 (i.e. not representing an actual WW1 pilot/aircraft). The aircraft was displayed at Hood Aerodrome in this colour scheme on one or two occasions before being converted back to Lothar's accurate colour scheme.

Year: 1917 *Built:* 320 *Top Speed:* 185km/h *Operational Ceiling:* 6100m *Wingspan:* 7.19m *Height:* 2.95m *Length:* 5.77m
Max Weight: 586kg *Engine:* 110hp Oberursel UR.II rotary *Climb:* 5.7m/s *Range:* 300km *Armament:* 2 x 7.92mm Spandau LMG
This Aircraft: Replica with a 165hp 7-cylinder air cooled Warner Scarab radial engine, built in the USA. ZK-FOT

Facing Page Pilot: Tim Sullivan

Fokker Dr.1 'Triplane'

155 / 17 Lt Eberhardt Mohnicke

Initially assigned to a tactical bomber unit (*Kaghol 2*) Mohnicke scored his first victory while flying with that unit during 1916. In May 1917 he transferred to Jasta 11, and it was there that he scored the remainder of his nine victories. He went on to become CO of Jasta 11 on three separate occasions up until the time he was wounded in September 1918.

He was also wounded on the 1st March 1918 (presumably) while flying this aircraft, though reports note the Dr.1 itself was unharmed. The aircraft remained in service with Jasta 11 until late April at least and it is thought to have been used by another pilot as well as Mohnicke.

A symbol with ancient origins, the left facing swastika on the aircraft was widely used in Britain, Europe and America in the early part of the 20th Century as a symbol of good luck.

Since WW2 the symbol is often attributed to Nazism and right wing politics, with the result that many Westerners do not know of, or understand its pre-Nazi and historical use.

Year: 1917 *Built:* 320 *Top Speed:* 185km/h *Operational Ceiling:* 6100m *Wingspan:* 7.19m *Height:* 2.95m *Length:* 5.77m
Max Weight: 586kg *Engine:* 110hp Oberursel UR.II rotary *Climb:* 5.7m/s *Range:* 300km *Armament:* 2 x 7.92mm Spandau LMG
This Aircraft: Replica with a 165hp 7-cylinder air cooled Warner Scarab radial engine, built in the USA. *[OAHC]* ZK-JOB

Facing Page Pilot: John Bargh

Fokker Dr.1 'Triplane'

588 / 17 Lt Richard Wenzl

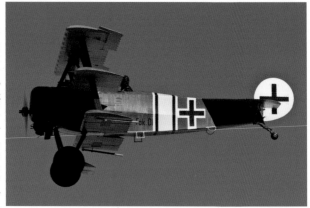

Wenzl's personal aircraft marking consisted of a white and black fuselage band in the same proportions as the Iron Cross ribbon, but with the colours reversed. Additionally the leading edge of the wings were painted in alternating black and white stripes.

Wenzl's first two victories were in April and May 1917 while he flew with Jasta 31, but he did not have another victory (an S.E.5a) until 16th May 1918.

Some attribute this victory to Jasta 11, while others note it was scored after Wenzl had transferred to Jasta 6. He subsequently went on to survive the war with a total of twelve victories, including a balloon that he shot down in the vicinity of Croiselles.

Wenzl was a good friend of Jasta 6 CO Johann Janzen, and by personal request he was transferred to this unit on the 15th May 1918. Despite having transferred to a new unit, over the next few weeks Wenzl continued to live with his comrade Werner Steinhäuser of Jasta 11.

For a short period from 11th August to the 1st Sept 1918 Wenzl was the Commanding Officer of Jasta 6.

Year: 1917 *Built:* 320 *Top Speed:* 185km/h *Operational Ceiling:* 6100m *Wingspan:* 7.19m *Height:* 2.95m *Length:* 5.77m
Max Weight: 586kg *Engine:* 110hp Oberursel UR.II rotary *Climb:* 5.7m/s *Range:* 300km *Armament:* 2 x 7.92mm Spandau LMG
This Aircraft: Replica with a 165hp 7-cylinder air cooled Warner Scarab radial engine, built in the USA. ZK-JOG

Facing Page Pilot: Greg MacDonald

Fokker Dr.1 'Triplane'

Unidentified aircraft and pilot

This aircraft represents another of the Jasta 11 triplanes flown by that unit in late April 1918.

Original photographs of this Dr.1 exist, but there is no record as to who piloted the aircraft, nor what the construction number was.

This aircraft was also temporarily 'made up' with fictional colours for the filming of the Australian War Memorial Museum film. In this case the white parts of the personal markings were replaced with yellow, as shown in the inset photo at centre right. After the filming was complete the aircraft was displayed in this scheme on several occasions in 2008 & 2009.

Year: 1917   *Built:* 320   *Top Speed:* 185km/h   *Operational Ceiling:* 6100m   *Wingspan:* 7.19m   *Height:* 2.95m   *Length:* 5.77m
Max Weight: 586kg   *Engine:* 110hp Oberursel UR.II rotary   *Climb:* 5.7m/s   *Range:* 300km   *Armament:* 2 x 7.92mm Spandau LMG
This Aircraft: Replica with a 165hp 7-cylinder air cooled Warner Scarab radial engine, built in the USA.   ZK-JOK

Facing Page Pilot: Paul Hughan

Pfalz D.III

4011 / 17 Lt Fritz Höhn

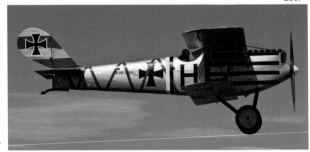

The D.III was the first aircraft of its own design to be built by Pfalz Flugzeug-Werk as the company had previously been building Roland-designed fighters under licence. Used from late 1917 the type reached its peak in April 1918 when over 430 examples of the D.III and D.IIIA were at the front.

This aircraft is another D.III built for the 1966 movie *The Blue Max*. The first aircraft was of all wood construction and was built by the Hampshire Airplane Club. This aircraft was built by Personal Plane Services, and was based on a Gypsy or Tiger Moth steel tube fuselage.

Fritz Höhn started the war as a soldier in the 7th Guards Infantry Regiment before switching to the air service. He initially flew two-seaters, but joined Jasta 21s and switched to fighters in November 1917.

While flying the Pfalz Höhn began to specialise in attacks on Allied kite balloons. By the time he was killed in October 1918 he had amassed a total of 21 victories, which included ten balloons.

The black and white stripe on the fuselage are the standard markings for Jasta 21s, while the rest of the colour scheme are Höhn's own markings. He believed that the red spiral ribbons would help break up the profile of the aircraft and make it difficult for enemy gunners to hit.

Year: 1917 *Built:* 1010 *Top Speed:* 185 km/h *Operational Ceiling:* 5200m *Wingspan:* 9.4m *Height:* 2.67m *Length:* 6.95m
Max Weight: 935kg *Engine:* 160hp Mercedes D.III water cooled inline *Climb:* 2.33 m/s *Endurance:* 150 mins *Armament:* 2 x 7.92mm Spandau LMG 08/15 *This Aircraft:* Replica with a 6-cylinder 200hp Gipsy Queen, built in the UK (was N906AC). *ZK-FLZ*

Facing Page Pilot: Stuart Tantrum

Fokker D.VII

4524 /18 - Lt. Johann Janzen, Jasta 6

Introduced in May 1918 the D.VII quickly developed a reputation as one of the finest single-seat fighters of the war.

Jasta 10 was the first unit to receive the type, while Jasta 11 received theirs only a few short weeks after Manfred von Richthofen had been killed in his Fokker Dr.1 in April.

This aircraft is painted in the colours of Lt Johann Janzen, a cavalry officer who transferred to the German Army Air Service (Luftstreitkräfte) in May 1916.

By March 1918 Janzen had scored four victories and was given command of Jasta 4 Following the death of von Richthofen in April, the CO of Jasta 6 (Reinhard) was promoted to command of Jagdgeschwader 1, and Janzen returned to Jasta 6 to take command. The unit received their D.VIIs in mid-May, and on the 20th Janzen shot down his first aircraft from a D.VII (a Sopwith Dolphin of 23 Sqn).

He remained CO of the unit, shooting down another nine aircraft (for a total of 13) until he was taken prisoner on 9th June. He was forced to land behind British lines when an interrupter malfunction caused him to shoot off his own propeller.

Janzen's personal aircraft markings consisted of a 'white snake' line on a black band, edged in white around the rear fuselage. He also used this emblem on the Fokker Dr.1 he flew up until Jasta 6 was re-equipped with the Fokker D.VII. The black and white stripes on the nose and tail of this aircraft were common to all Jasta 6 aircraft.

This particular aircraft is one of three replica Fokker D.VIIs built for the movie *The Blue Max* in the late 1960s.

Year: 1918 *Built:* approx 1700 *Top Speed:* 186 km/h *Operational Ceiling:* 5970m *Wingspan:* 8.09m *Height:* 2.75m *Length:* 6.95m *Max Weight:* 850kg *Engine:* 160hp Mercedes D.III water cooled inline *Climb:* 4 m/s *Endurance:* 90 mins *Armament:* 2 x 7.92mm Spandau *This Aircraft:* Replica with a 6-cylinder 200hp Gipsy Queen, built by Rosseau Aviation (France). *ZK-FOD*

Facing Page Pilot: Stuart Tantrum

Nieuport 11

Ni. 2123 Sgt Alvaro Leonardi

Designed as a contender in the 1914 Gordon Bennett air race, the N.11 was small, fast and highly maneuverable. After the race was cancelled due to the outbreak of the war, it was not long before France's *Aviation Militaire* accepted it for production as a combat aircraft.

The N.11 (along with the Airco DH.2 and RAF F.E.8 'pushers') was effective at countering the *'Fokker Scourge'* of 1916 when the German Fokker E.III monoplanes had gained significant superiority over the earlier Allied aircraft designs

Assigned to the 80a Squadriglia, Italian Air Service in May 1917, N.2123 was one of the 646 N.11s built under license by the Italian company Maachi. The aircraft became the personal mount of Sgt. Alvaro Leonardi, who ended the war with a score of eight victories. The only one of those gained at the controls of Ni. 2123 was scored in May 1917, when he shot down a Ufag L1 seaplane.

The emblem on the fuselage was based on the Italian version of the 'Happy Hooligan' comic strip, in which the character was called 'Fortunello' (meaning 'Lucky'). He is reminiscent of the modern day Homer Simpson.

Year: 1915 *Built:* 700+ *Top Speed:* 156 km/h *Operational Ceiling:* 4600m *Wingspan:* 7.55m *Height:* 2.45m *Length:* 5.8m
Max Weight: 480kg *Engine:* 80hp Le Rhône 9C rotary *Range:* 330km *Endurance:* 150 mins *Armament:* 1 x .303 Lewis or Hotchkiss firing above the propeller *This Aircraft:* Replica with an original 80hp Le Rhône rotary, built in the USA. ZK-NIM

Facing Page Pilot: John Lanham

Royal Aircraft Factory S.E.5a

F5690 - Pilot Unknown

The S.E.5 ("Scout Experimental 5") was designed around the new 150-hp Hispano-Suiza 8a V8 engine. The first two were lost in crashes due to a weak wing but the third underwent significant modification, and the type ultimately became known as a very strong machine that could be dived at high speed.

The first examples of the aircraft were delivered to the RFC before the Sopwith Camel, but on-going problems with the engine meant there were relatively few S.E.5s in service until well into 1918.

The introduction of the 200-hp Hispano-Suiza or Wolseley Viper (a version of the Hispano-Suiza made under license) resolved the engine problems and added nearly 45 km/hour to the aircraft's top speed.

The colour scheme of this aircraft is that of a Presentation Aircraft given to the Royal Flying Corps. Other than the original photo (at right) and some evidence that it was still in service with the Royal Air Force in 1919, little is known about F5690's service history. The legend on the fuselage reads:

"Wanganui"
Presented by
Mr E.R. Jackson
Wanganui
New Zealand

Year: 1917 *Built:* 5205 *Top Speed:* 222 km/h *Operational Ceiling:* 5944m *Wingspan:* 8.11m *Height:* 2.89m *Length:* 6.38m
Max Weight: 902kg *Engine:* 200hp Wolseley Viper water cooled V12 *Range:* 483km *Endurance:* 180 mins *Armament:* 1 x .303
Vickers + 1 x .303 Lewis on upper wing. *This Aircraft:* New TVAL reproduction with license built 180hp Hispano Suiza.   ZK-SEV

Facing Page Pilot: Gene De Marco

Bristol Fighter F.2b

D-8084 - No 139 Sqn, RAF, Italy 1918

Brought into New Zealand in 2006 this Bristol Fighter was one of several original airframes that were found to be part of the structure of a mezzanine floor in an Oxfordshire (UK) barn in the 1960s. The aircraft was rebuilt and made it's first post restoration flight in 1998 and it currently sports the oldest airworthy Rolls Royce aero engine in the world.

The original constructors number (7434) was found on a number of components of this aircraft during the restoration and this enabled it to be identified as F-4516 which originally flew with 13 Sqn, RFC.

The aircraft now wears the colour scheme of D-8084. That aircraft flew with No 139 Sqn RAF while based at Villaverla in Italy late in 1918. In addition to supporting their Italian allies in the defence of Italy during the Austro-German invasion, the aircraft was also used by HRH Prince Edward of Wales (later Edward the VIII) when he visited the squadron and flew in the aircraft as an observer.

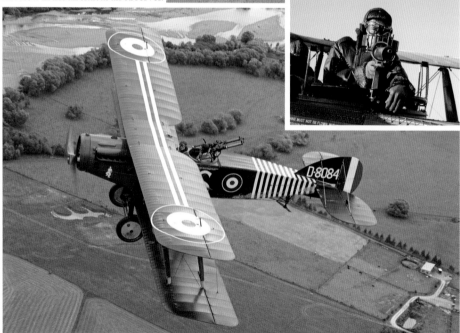

Year: 1917	Built: 5329	Top Speed: 198 km/h	Operational Ceiling: 5500m	Wingspan: 11.96m	Height: 2.97m	Length: 7.87m

Max Weight: 1261kg   Engine: 275hp Rolls Royce Falcon III v12   Climb: 4.5m/s   Range: 593km   Endurance: 180mins   Armament: 1 x .303 Vickers and 1 or 2 x Lewis in rear + up to 110kg bombs   This Aircraft: Original with original RR Falcon engine.   ZK-BRI

Facing Page Pilot: Gene De Marco

Breguet 14 B2

US 96th Aero Squadron

The Breguet 14 was one of the first mass produced aircraft to use large amounts of metal (duralumin) in its construction instead of wood. This resulted in a aircraft that was lighter than it otherwise would be making it agile and fast for its size.

The A2 version was initially developed as a reconnaissance aircraft and by April 1917 over 500 of these aircraft were on order. The B2 variant was designed specifically as a bomber version and it differed from the earlier model by having bomb racks and the transparent side panels in the observers cockpit.

The type equipped 71 French units on the Western Front and were also deployed in considerable numbers in Serbia, Morocco, Greece and Macedonia. The American Expeditionary Force used over 350 examples of the two variants (plus an unarmed training model).

Following the end of the war the type continued to see military and civilian service, and production did not end until 1928. In 1919 two Frenchmen (Roget and Coli) made the first double crossing of the Mediterranean Sea in a Breguet 14, while around 70 of the type were used duing the Polish-Soviet war between 1919 and 1921. Later they were also supplied to over a dozen foreign air forces in Europe, South America and the Far East. The last examples used by the French military were withdrawn from service in 1932.

The US 96th Aero Squadron was formed in June 1918 and until November that year was based in France supporting the French Eighth and US First Armies. The unit still exists today as the 96th Bomb Squadron and since 1993 has operated the B-52 Stratofortress.

Year: 1917 *Built: ca* 7800 *Top Speed:* 175 km/h *Operational Ceiling:* 5800m *Wingspan:* 14.86m *Height:* 3.3m *Length:* 8.87m *Max Weight:* 1536kg *Engine:* 300hp Renault 12Fcx water cooled *Range:* 900km *Climb:* 4.8m/s *Endurance:* 165 mins *Armament:* 1 x .303 Vickers fixed, 2 x .303 Lewis for observer, up to 300kg bombs *This Aircraft:* Static replica only. *[OAHC]*

Royal Aircraft Factory S.E.5a
B507 - 2nd/Lt J.J. Fitzgerald

The S.E.5 was first used in action by No 56 Squadron RFC on the 22nd April 1917. By the end of 1917 a further seven RFC squadrons had been equipped with the type which by then had developed into the '5a' variant (with a 200hp engine instead of the earlier 150hp Hispano-Suiza).

Throughout 1916 and 1917 the number of British aircraft operating in France rose dramatically. In order to be able to identify the units that specific aircraft belonged to the RFC began issuing orders for units to paint various geometrical shapes on the fuselages of their aircraft. In late August 1917 a new set of orders was released, with details of updated unit markings.

The unit markings for No 60 Squadron was to become a white circle painted on the sides of the fuselage behind the roundel, and also on the top of the fuselage behind the cockpit. These markings remained in force until the German Army launched an offensive on the Western Front on the 21st of March 1918. The following day (in an attempt to confuse the Germans) all RFC two seater units were ordered to paint out their unit markings, while all fighter squadrons swapped their markings around. Subsequently the markings for No 60 Sqn became (and remained for the rest of the war) a pair of white bands around the fuselage, just forward of the tail.

This S.E.5a represents that of B507 'A', an aircraft of A Flight, No 60 Sqn. On the 5th October 1917, 2nd/Lt J.J. Fitzgerald was forced to land behind enemy lines (thus becoming a POW in the process) due to engine failure while flying this aircraft. Captured intact, the aircraft was then examined and photographed in detail by the Germans.

Year: 1917 Built: 5205 Top Speed: 193 km/h Operational Ceiling: 5944m Wingspan: 8.11m Height: 2.89m Length: 6.38m Max Weight: 902kg Engine: 200hp Wolesley Viper water cooled V12 Range: 483km Endurance: 180 mins Armament: 1 x .303 Vickers + 1 x .303 Lewis on upper wing. This Aircraft: New TVAL reproduction with license built 180hp Hispano Suiza. ZK-SEO

Facing Page Pilot: Gene De Marco

Royal Aircraft Factory S.E.5a

D3540 'K' - Capt Gwilym H. Lewis

By the time the engine-related production problems of the S.E.5a had been solved in early 1918, the aircraft had acquired a reputation of having excellent flying qualities and performance, along with considerable strength.

Remaining in service through until the end of the war the type is usually credited, along with the Sopwith Camel, of helping the Allies regain air superiority over the Western Front during 1918.

By the end of the war, the S.E.5a had been used to equip 24 RFC squadrons, two American units, and one Australian squadron.

Until March 1918, the unit symbols used by No 40 Sqn RFC consisted of three white bands around the fuselage—two just forward of the tail, and one behind the cockpit. On the 22nd March 1918 the unit started to use an 'N' shaped flash forward of the tail, usually inclining toward the front of the aircraft.

Captain Gwilym Hugh Lewis ended the war with a total of 12 victories to his credit, at least four of which were scored while flying D3540. On 11th April 1918 he shot down a Fokker Dr.1, and over the course of the next six weeks shot down three Pfalz D.III fighters while flying this aircraft.

Year: 1917 *Built:* 5205 *Top Speed:* 193 km/h *Operational Ceiling:* 5944m *Wingspan:* 8.11m *Height:* 2.89m *Length:* 6.38m *Max Weight:* 902kg *Engine:* 200hp Wolesley Viper water cooled V12 *Range:* 483km *Endurance:* 180 mins *Armament:* 1 x .303 Vickers + 1 x .303 Lewis on upper wing. *This Aircraft*: New TVAL reproduction, with license built 180hp Hispano Suiza.   ZK-SES

Fokker D.VII

7871/18

The D.VII was initially powered by a 180hp Mercedes D.III engine but these were soon replaced with a 200hp Mercedes and then an 'over-compressed' 185hp BMW IIIa engine which gave the aircraft even better performance.

By the end of the war 775 aircraft of this type were still in service with over 46 Jagdstafflen (fighter squadrons)—this being more than twice the total number of Fokker Dr.1 Triplanes that had been built.

The type was so respected by the Allies that it was specifically mentioned in the Armistice agreements—Germany had to surrender all D.VII aircraft. This confiscation of the aircraft led the D.VII to be used all over the world by many countries after the war. Examples were still in use by Switzerland, The Netherlands and Lithuania into the late 1930s.

Despite the requirement to hand over all the aircraft to the Allies, some pilots flew their aircraft back to Germany.Anthony Fokker smuggled six trains with sixty wagons each full of aeroplanes and tools into Holland—among these were 120 Fokker D.VIIs.

This particular aircraft is one of three replica D.VIIs built for the movie *The Blue Max* in the mid-1960s. Built in a short space of time, the aircraft looked like a Fokker D.VII, but the materials and construction methods were very different, and its performance was not up to that expected of an original D.VII. After displaying the replica at several New Zealand airshows, The Vintage Aviator decided to spend some time working on the aircraft. After removing over 135kg of excess weight, redesigning the nose and undercarriage the aircraft not only looks better but also performs more like the highly regarding fighter aircraft of the First World War.

Year: 1918 *Built:* ca 1700 *Top Speed:* 186 km/h *Operational Ceiling:* 5970m *Wingspan:* 8.09m *Height:* 2.75m *Length:* 6.95m
Max Weight: 850kg *Engine:* 160hp Mercedes D.III water cooled inline *Climb:* 4 m/s *Endurance:* 90 mins *Armament:* 2 x
7.92mm Spandau *This Aircraft:* Replica with a 6-cylinder 200hp Gipsy Queen, built by Rosseau Aviation (France). *ZK-FOD*

Facing Page Pilot: Jerry Chisum

Sopwith Triplane

N533 - Lt Raymond Collishaw, RNAS

In early 1916 Sopwith produced the 'Pup', a biplane aircraft with exceptional maneuverability and performance—the ideal characteristics of a fighter aircraft. In an attempt to better this the designers at Sopwith added an additional wing, and produced the Triplane.

The outstanding climb rate and agility of the new type so impressed the German aircraft designers that over two dozen German triplane designs were soon developed. The most well known and successful of these being the Dr.1 developed by Fokker.

The Triplane was operated exclusively by the Royal Naval Air Service (RNAS) until its replacement by the Sopwith Camel in the summer of 1917.

The colour scheme of this aircraft is that of one of several Triplanes named 'Black Maria' flown by Canadian ace Lt Raymond Collishaw. Flying with No 10 Naval Sqd, RNAS. Collishaw was the third highest British ace, ending the war with a total of 60 victories. In 1919 he increased his tally to 62 while commanding No 47 Sqn RAF during the Russian Civil War.

*Year:* 1916 *Built:* 147 *Top Speed:* 188 km/h *Operational Ceiling:* 6250m *Wingspan:* 8.08m *Height:* 3.2m *Length:* 5.73m
Max Weight: 642 kg *Engine:* 130hp Clerget 9B rotary *Climb:* 5 m/s *Range:* 450km *Endurance:* 165 mins *Armament:* 1 or (rarely) 2 x .303 Vickers *This Aircraft:* Replica with 165hp Warner Scarab engine, USA project completed by TVAL. *ZK-SOP*

Facing Page Pilot: John Bargh

Royal Aircraft Factory B.E.2f

A1325 - Generic Royal Flying Corps colour scheme

The original "Blériot Experimental 2" was designed in 1912 by Geoffrey de Havilland and was the first British aircraft designed specifically for military use. While Louis Blériot had been designing aircraft for some time, these RAF aircraft had no connection with his designs—the naming convention was simply designed to indicate that they were general purpose two-seat tractor biplanes.

The first B.E.2s were delivered to the Royal Flying Corps in 1913, and by the outbreak of war in July 1914 they were in service with three RFC squadrons. The design was inherently stable, and while this made them easy to fly, it also made them virtually helpless against the more maneuverable German fighters (particularly the Fokker E.I/III).

Additionally the back-to-front seating arrangement where the observer sat in the front, between the two wings and amongst the rigging, usually made it difficult for him to bring his guns to bear on any opponents.

In 1916 the Royal Aircraft Factory tried to improve upon the previous B.E.2 designs by developing the 'e' model which featured wings of unequal span and a single pair of interplane struts. Some older B.E.2c aircraft (previously with wings of equal span) were converted to this new variant, and they were designated the B.E.2f. These changes did little to enhance the combat effectiveness of the aircraft and by the end of the war most B.E.2s were relegated to a training role only.

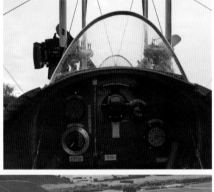

This aircraft (A1325) is one of 17 RFC veterans shipped to Norway in 1917 and is a genuine WW1 survivor. The aircraft was restored by The Vintage Aviator Ltd, and made its maiden post-restoration flight in 2009.

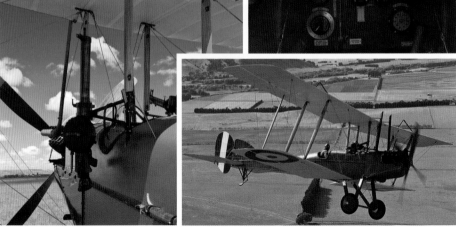

Year: 1916 Built: 3500+ *(all B.E.2 variants)* Top Speed: 132 km/h Operational Ceiling: 3048m Wingspan: 12.42m Height: 3.66m
Length: 8.31m Engine: 90hp R.A.F.1a air cooled V-8 Range: 320km Endurance: 240mins Armament: 1 or 2 x .303 Lewis with up to 102kg bombs This Aircraft: TVAL-restored original with a TVAL-built 90hp R.A.F.1a engine reproduction. ZK-BFR

Facing Page Pilot: John Bargh

Avro 504k

Generic 1914 RFC Colour Scheme

The 504 is a significant part of aviation history in New Zealand. Of the twenty 504s supplied to NZ by Britain in 1920, 18 were loaned to commercial companies who were beginning the post-war development of aviation (the other two were retained by the Government). Later, the New Zealand Permanent Air Force re-acquired some of these aircraft, as well as purchasing six more, and used them throughout the remainder of the 1920s as training aircraft.

In August 1920, Capt Euan Dickson (a WW1 ace), used a 504 to make the first aerial crossing of Cook Strait between New Zealand's North and South Islands), starting from a field just outside Blenheim .

The aircraft shown here is one of the most historic original aircraft surviving in New Zealand. This 504 has been flown (as recorded in the aircraft's original log books) by such pioneer aviators as Chichester, Hood, Moncrief, McGregor and the Australians, Kingsford-Smith and Ulm.

Year: 1913 *Built:* 8970 *Top Speed:* 145km/h *Operational Ceiling:* 4875m *Wingspan:* 10.979m *Height:* 3.17m *Length:* 8.97m
Max Weight: 830kg *Engine:* 110-130hp Clerget rotary *Climb:* 3.6m/s *Range:* 402km *Endurance:* 165mins *Armament:* Provision for four 9kg Cooper bombs *This Aircraft:* Restored original with a 100hp Gnome 9-cylinder rotary engine. ZK-ACU

Royal Aircraft Factory F.E.2b

*6341 - Zanzibar No.1/Scotch Express,
No. 25 Sqd RFC. Capt. Douglas Grinnell-
Milne & Corp. D. MacMaster.*

A two-seat fighter/reconnaissance aircraft, the 'Farman Experimental 2' pusher was almost obsolete in this role by the time it reached the front in numbers in early 1916, due in most part to the rapid improvement in German fighter aircraft designs.

At its peak 16 Royal Flying Corps squadrons were using the type. The fighter model ('d' variant) was withdrawn from combat in April 1917, but the 'b' variant was used as a night bomber until August 1918.

This TVAL-built reproduction features a number of original F.E.2b parts (interplane struts, oil and fuel tanks, radiator shutter, wheels and the Beardmore engine amongst other parts). The aircraft was also built with original techniques and materials such as Irish linen and ash and spruce timbers.

On 16 May 1916 the original *Scotch Express* was forced down behind enemy lines by Ltn Gontermann of Jasta 5. It was then photographed by its captors and this evidence allowed TVAL to reproduce the colour scheme with a high degree of accuracy.

Year: 1915 *Built:* 1939 *Top Speed:* 147 km/h *Operational Ceiling:* 3353m *Wingspan:* 14.55m *Height:* 3.85m *Length:* 9.83m
Max Weight: 1380kg *Engine:* 120h/160p Beardmore water cooled V-12 *Climb:* 1.3 m/s *Endurance:* 150 mins *Armament:*
1 or 2 x .303 Lewis & up to 235kg bombs *This Aircraft:* New TVAL reproduction with original 160hp Beardmore engine. *ZK-FEE*

Facing Page Pilot: Gene De Marco

Royal Aircraft Factory B.E.2c

347 - 1914 RFC colour scheme

In October 1914 several B.E.2c's, including aircraft '347', were the first British aircraft to arrive in France. However the first fully equipped B.E.2 squadron (No. 8) did not arrive until April 1915.

The B.E.2c was produced in greater numbers than all the other models and featured the innovation of ailerons on both upper and lower wings which replaced wing-warping controls used on the 'a' and 'b' models.

Early B.E.2c's were powered by a 70hp Renault engine and featured undercarriage landing skids often employed on early aircraft. Later 'c' models were powered by 90hp R.A.F.1a engines and those variants dispensed with the landing skids. The earlier aircraft could only carry up to 45kg of bombs.

The colour scheme of this aircraft is that of '347' as seen in France up until December 1914 (when roundels replaced the Union Jack on British aircraft).

Year: 1914 *Built:* 3500+ *(all B.E.2 variants)* *Top Speed:* 116 km/h *Operational Ceiling:* 3048m *Wingspan:* 11.28m *Height:* 3.4m *Length:* 8.31m *Engine:* 70hp Renault air cooled V-8 *Range:* approx 300km *Endurance:* 195mins *Armament:* No fixed guns but up to 45kg bombs *This Aircraft:* New TVAL reproduction aircraft with an original 80hp Renault engine. *ZK-TVA*

Facing Page Pilot: Gene De Marco

Albatros D.Va

5284/17 - Vfw Josef Mai, Jasta 5

In 1916 most German aircraft manufacturers were directed to look at what made the Allied Nieuport fighters so effective, and to incorporate those elements into their new aircraft designs.

Albatros redesigned their D.II model as a sesquiplane, like the Nieuports, with a lower wing with a narrower chord width than the upper wing. The resulting D.III was a great new aircraft and established itself as a formidable fighter throughout 1917.

In mid-1917 the D.V/Va was an attempt to improve on the D.III to keep up with newly deployed Allied aircraft such as the R.A.F. S.E.5a and Sopwith Camel. The D.Va was strengthened and had a streamlined oval fuselage instead of the flat sided one of the D.III. However, these and other minor changes were not enough to keep the D.Va at the forefront of fighter technology.

By early 1918 the D.III and D.Va were being replaced at the front by new Fokker Dr.1s and then D.VIIs. Despite this the aircraft remained in active service through until the Armistice in November 1918.

Mai scored 11 victories flying Albatros fighters (seven in this aircraft) before moving to the Fokker fighters. He ended the war with a tally of 30 confirmed victories.

Year: 1917 *Built:* approx 2500 *Top Speed:* 187 km/h *Operational Ceiling:* 6250m *Wingspan:* 9.05m *Height:* 2.85m *Length:* 7.33m
Max Weight: 937kg *Engine:* 170/185hp Mercedes D.IIIa water cooled 6 cylinder inline *Climb:* 4.5m/s *Endurance:* 120 mins
Armament: 2 x 7.92mm machine guns *This Aircraft:* New TVAL reproduction with original Mercedes D.III engine. *ZK-DVA*

Facing Page Pilot: Gene De Marco

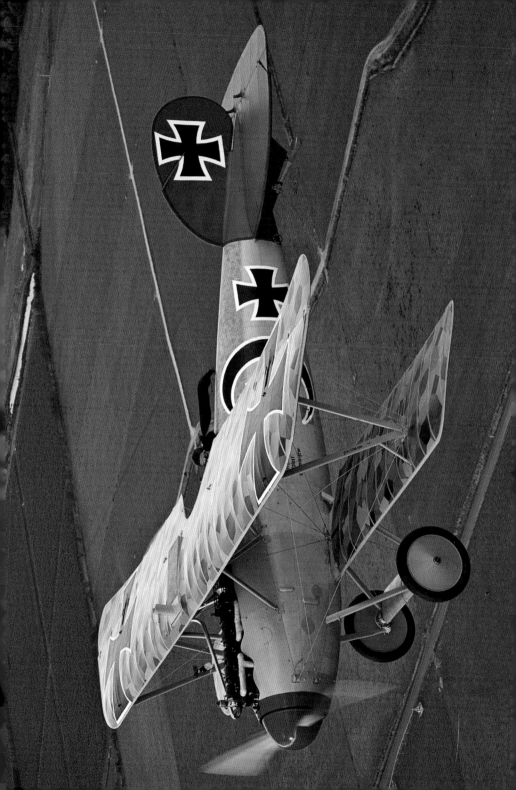

Wings Of War Gaming

Wings of War is a modular boardgame collection representing air combat, both in the First and Second World Wars. The game mixes card game, board game, and miniature gaming mechanics to simulate air combat in the 20th century.

The mechanics of the game are very simple to learn and an enjoyable game with up to three of four participants can be played out in 30 minutes or less, on any table or other flat surface.

Each aircraft type is depicted on a playing card and each has its own specific deck of Maneuver Cards. Each player controlling an aircraft plans his turn choosing three Maneuver Cards in sequence and puts them face down on the gaming mat. All players simultaneously reveal their first card for the turn, put it in front of the aircraft and move the Aircraft Card so that the small arrows on the rear of the card matches the one at the front of the Maneuver Card.

A ruler is used to see if a plane has enemy cards in his field of fire: if so, the player chooses one target aircraft which then takes a Damage Card with a random amount of points (optional rules cover special damages too). The various maneuvers available to a pilot player, the aircraft firepower and number of damage points sustained before the aircraft is shot down depends on the type of aircraft being used.

Each of the first three box sets of the World War One series allow two to four people to play, and sets can be combined to allow for more participants in each game. The sets are:

Famous Aces: this includes a selection of fighters with personal colours of the most renowned aces of World War I: the aircraft types are Fokker Dr.I and Albatros D.Va for Central Powers and the SPAD XIII, Sopwith Camel and Sopwith Triplane for the Allies.

Watch your back!: adding new fighter types and some two-seaters, this set allows bombings, reconnaissance missions and other special scenarios.

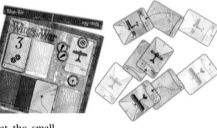

Burning Drachens: includes observation balloons (drachans), AA guns, machine guns, air-to-air Le Prieur rockets, trench systems, and optional altitude rules. This set also includes rules for solo play as well as multi-player dogfights, bombing runs, and strafing or reconnaissance missions.

A variety of Booster packs are available which add new aircraft types to the game. The *Immelmann* booster allows players to use famous early war aircraft such as the Fokker

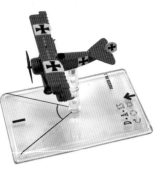

Eindecker, Airco DH.2 and Morane-Saulnier Type N while the *Dogfight* booster adds new high performance later-war aircraft such as the R.A.F. S.E.5a and Siemens-Schuckert D.III and D.IV fighters.

The game can be played solely as a card/board game, or can be enhanced by using the complimentary 1/144th scale miniatures that are available. These are made of pre-painted pewter and plastic and come with a gaming base and a set of maneuver cards. A number of different miniatures have been released, and the range is continually expanding.

A Second World War version of the Wings of War game system is also available, although the mechanics of the game vary in order to accommodate the increase in aircraft speed and firepower during WW2, so these cannot be mixed with the WW1 sets.

Wings of War is published by Nexus Editrice and Fantasy Flight Games (English Edition) and is available in New Zealand from good game stockists and the Historical Aviation Film Unit: *www.aviationfilm.com/shop/games/*

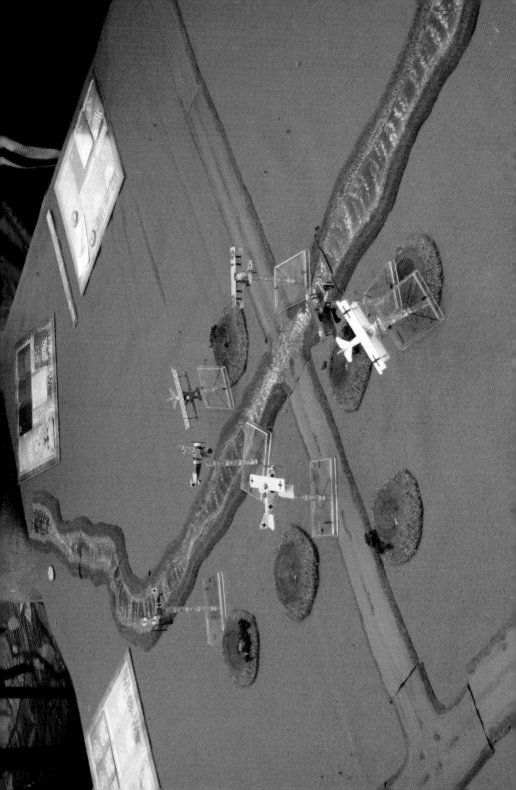

Wingnut Wings: High Quality Model Kitsets

Wingnut Wings has a passion to provide accurate, highly detailed 1/32nd scale models that are enjoyable to build for both experienced and novice modelers alike. With these kits the company hopes to attract people previously unaccustomed to the satisfaction of modelling aviation's epic and tragic pioneer years.

In the short time these aircraft patrolled the war torn skies over the trenches they represented the cutting edge of technology. In keeping with that tradition Wingnut Wings use the latest in 3D CAD/CAM modelling software and tool making techniques available to ensure that they make only the highest quality product.

Designed and researched by passionate professionals utilising original factory drawings whenever possible, historic and contemporary photos, information supplied by some of the worlds leading experts in their fields and working closely with The Vintage Aviator Ltd, Wingnut Wings believe their models to be the most accurate ever produced of their subjects. All models require assembly, and paint and glue are not included.

The scale model aircraft available now include the Junkers J.1, LVG C.VI, R.A.F. S.E.5a, Bristol F.2b Fighter, Albatros D.V and D.Va and the Sopwith Pup (RFC & RNAS).

These kits are available exclusively from Wingnut Wings via the internet at: *www.wingnutwings.com*

Our Thanks To...

Over the last ten years there have been many people who have helped us in one way or another on our journey towards the final production of this book. This collection of photographs would not have been possible without this help, so we'd like to take this opportunity to say "Thank You" to you all.

World War I Aircraft Pilots

John Bargh	Jerry Chisum
Pete Cochrane	Gene De Marco
Stuart Goldspink	Dave Horrell
Paul Hughan	John Lanham
Greg MacDonald	Scott McKenzie
Fred Murrin	Frank Parker
Simon Paul	Steve Petersen
Jim Rankin	Keith Skilling
Tim Sullivan	Stuart Tantrum
Gavin Trethewey	Andrew Vincent
Gary Yardley	

Camera Ship Pilots

Wayne Allanson	Kerry Conner
Trevor Collins	Graeme Frew
Alastair Marshall	Jay McIntyre
Stephen Witte	

General Help & Support

Allan Baker	Chris Boyce
Wayne Bradley	Paul Buchannan
Joanna Carson	Dave Cretchley
Tracey Curtis	Craig Justo
Dave Lochead	David Marwick
Philip Merry	Marty Nicholl
Greg Olsen	Liz Pollock
Sara Randle	James Slade
Bevan Udy	Kris Whelan

... and the rest of the team of crafts men and women at The Vintage Aviator – well done!

Finally, but most importantly, we must thank the ever tolerant Karen and Janet, both of whom sacrificed much over the last decade while we have pursued our passion for old aircraft.

As always we sincerely apologise to anyone who we may have inadvertently omitted from this list. Let us know, and we'll shout you a drink the next time we catch up with you!

Alex Mitchell & Allan Udy
Historical Aviation Film Unit

Other Historical Aviation Film Unit Products

Visit the Historical Aviation Film Unit web site to subscribe to our periodic email newsletter, and to check out some of the other aviation related products we have available, including Collectors Postcards, Aviation DVD's, Wings of War miniatures and links to our YouTube video channel. See us at: *www.aviationfilm.com*

Accuracy Of Aircraft Data

This book is a pictorial guide and general introduction to the WW1-era aircraft of The Vintage Aviator and the 1914-1918 Aviation Heritage Trust. While efforts have been made to ensure that all data presented is accurate, historical data is sometimes sparse and sources sometimes conflict.

Any omissions and errors within this book are the sole responsibility of the Historical Aviation Film Unit and not The Vintage Aviator or the 1914-1918 Aviation Heritage Trust.

Display Aircraft At OAHC

Some aircraft shown in this book are displayed inside the Omaka Aviation Heritage Centre in Blenheim, New Zealand.

The aircraft on display in the OAHC at the time of writing are noted with *[OAHC]* in the specifications box at the bottom of each page, and an asterisk '*' in the list at right. Aircraft on display in the museum can and do change so for an up-to-date list, always check the museum website at *www.omaka.org.nz.*

Photos in this book which were taken inside the Heritage Centre are used with permission of the New Zealand Aviation Museum Trust.

Chronological Order

The order of the entries in this book (as shown in the Aircraft Index) may appear random, but there is a pattern—each aircraft is presented in roughly the chronological order of its first public appearance in New Zealand.

References

Aces And Aircraft Of World War 1
Campbell, Christopher 1981
Blandford Press Ltd   ISBN: 0907812627

Albatros Aces Of World War 1
Franks, Norman 2000
Osprey Publishing Ltd   ISBN: 1855329603

Bombers, Patrol and Reconnaissance
Aircraft 1914-1919 *Munson, K* 1968
Blandford Press Ltd   ISBN: 0713704845

British and Empire Aces Of World War 1
Shores, Christopher 2001
Osprey Publishing Ltd   ISBN: 1841763772

Classic Aircraft Of New Zealand
Russell, Stuart and Mitchell, Alex 2003
Reed Publishing Ltd ISBN: 0790008904

Early German Aces of World War 1
VanWyngarden, G & Dempsey, H 2006
Osprey Publishing   ISBN: 9781841769974

Encyclopedia of Military Aircraft
Jackson, Robert 2002
Parragon   ISBN: 0752581309

Fighters, Attack and Training
Aircraft 1914-1919 *Munson, K* 1968
Blandford Press Ltd ISBN: 0713704837

Fokker Dr.1 Aces Of World War 1
Franks, N & VanWyngarden, G 2001
Osprey Publishing Ltd   ISBN: 1841762237

Fokker D.VII Aces Of World War 1 - Part 1
Franks, N & VanWyngarden, G 2003
Osprey Publishing Ltd   ISBN: 1841765333

Fokker D.VII Aces Of World War 1 - Part 2
Franks, N & VanWyngarden, G 2004
Osprey Publishing Ltd   ISBN: 184176729

German Army Air Service in World War 1
Rimell, Raymond 1985
Arms and Armour Press   ISBN: 0853686947

Halberstadt Fighters, Classics of WW1
Aviation *Grosz, Peter M.* 1993
Albatros Productions Ltd (?)

Illustrated Encyclopedia Of Aircraft
(Magazine Series in 216 Parts) 1982-1985
Orbis Publishing Ltd   No ISSN

Jane's Fighting Aircraft Of World War 1
1990 Random House Group Ltd
ISBN: 1851703470

Nieuport Aces Of World War 1
Franks, Norman 2000
Osprey Publishing Ltd   ISBN: 1855329611

Pfalz Scout Aces Of World War 1
VanWyngarden, G 2006
Osprey Publishing Ltd   ISBN: 1841769983

RAF SE5a, A Windsock Datafile Special.
Bruce, J.M. 1993
Albatros Productions   ISBN: 0948414472

SE5/5a Aces of World War 1
Franks, Norman. 2007
Osprey Publishing ISBN: 9781846031809

SE5/SE5a Squadrons
Rogers, L.A. 2000
Albatros Productions   ISBN: 1902207343

Sopwith Camel Aces Of World War 1
Franks, Norman 2003
Osprey Publishing Ltd   ISBN: 1841765341

Sopwith Triplane Aces Of World War 1
Franks, Norman 2004
Osprey Publishing Ltd   ISBN: 184176728X

* On display at Omaka Aviation Heritage Centre
† Not included in this history at OAHC request

Facing Page Pilot: Keith Skilling